Dorothy McRae-McMahon is a minister in the  years, she was a minister with the Pitt Street Ur and then, for five years, the National Director fc a member of the World Council of Churches Wc Assembly and Moderator of the Worship Committee for the Harare Assembly. She now contributes to the Faith column of *The Age*, Melbourne, and is a co-editor of *The South Sydney Herald*.

Her community awards indicate her interests and concerns. She has received a Jubilee Medal from the Queen for her work with women in New South Wales (1977), an Australian Government Peace Award (1986), the Australian Human Rights Medal (1988), and an Honorary Doctorate of Letters from Macquarrie University in Sydney for work with minorities and her contribution to the spiritual life of the community (1992).

ALSO BY THE AUTHOR

Being Clergy, Staying Human
(Alban Institute, Washington, Australia, 1992)

Echoes of Our Journey: Liturgies of the People
(Joint Board of Christian Education, Melbourne, 1993)

The Glory of Blood, Sweat and Tears: Liturgies for Living and Dying
(Joint Board of Christian Education, Melbourne, 1996)

Everyday Passions: A Conversation on Living
(ABC Books, Sydney, 1998)

Liturgies for the Journey of Life
(SPCK, 2000)

Prayers for Life's Particular Moments
(SPCK and Desbooks, 2001)

Daring Leadership in the 21st Century
(ABC Books, Sydney, 2001)

In This Hour: Liturgies for Pausing
(SPCK and Desbooks, 2002)

Rituals for Life, Love and Loss
(Jane Curry Publishing, 2003)

Memoirs of Moving On
(Jane Curry Publishing, 2004)

Liturgies for Daily Life
(SPCK, 2004)

Liturgies for High Days
(SPCK, 2006)

Liturgies for the Young in Years
(SPCK, 2007)

LITURGIES FOR THE YOUNG IN YEARS

DOROTHY McRAE-McMAHON

First published in Australia in 2005
as *Worship for the Young in Years*
by MediaCom Education Inc.

This edition first published in Great Britain in 2007

Society for Promoting Christian Knowledge
36 Causton Street
London SW1P 4ST

British Library Cataloguing-in-Publication Data
A catalogue record for this book is available from the British Library

ISBN-13: 978–0–281–05789–4

10 9 8 7 6 5 4 3 2 1

Design by Melanie Bartholomaeus
Printed in Great Britain by Ashford Colour Press

CONTENTS

INTRODUCTION

Many of these liturgies are based on work done during my time as a temporary chaplain with MLC (Methodists Ladies College) in Burwood, Sydney, Australia. However, I believe that they are also suitable for worship for children and young people in any setting. MLC is a school of the Uniting Church in Australia and as such uses contemporary liturgy based mostly on the lectionary readings from the *Revised Common Lectionary*.

The worship encourages students to become familiar with some of the traditional responses of the church in its worship life and gradually accustoms them to understanding the elements within a traditional service of worship. I found that they, particularly the younger children, loved to say the responses and entered into the 'mood' of each part of the liturgy with great sensitivity. Their Thanks be to God! and Amens! would put most adult congregations to shame! The liturgies are in written and responsive form so that those who can read can participate and some can lead. It could easily be adapted simply to being led by different people without the responses being used or by using them as prompts.

In some cases, I have included the main points of the reflection (sermon) after the readings in order to give more information about the theme of the liturgy and perhaps in the hope of saving the time of hard-pressed people who care for our young!

While MLC is a school run by the Christian church, it has many children of other faiths or none and is careful to be respectful of those students, while holding to its commitment to teach the Christian faith.

The services are for age groups from five to eighteen years old. I have assigned them to the different age groups but obviously this is only approximate. There are some services which the students shared with their parents. The senior students of MLC chose the themes for these services. There is also one in which the parents of new students passed on the 'mantle of care' to the staff of the school as they entrusted their children to the school. There is another which we prepared for the staff as they began a new school year and welcomed new staff. Both these services could be used in relation to Sunday school or youth group staff and/or parents.

The girls of MLC were my inspiration in preparing these liturgies. Their authentic responses to life and faith in their different years of journeying sometimes reminded me of an honesty which so many of us as adults have compromised or laid aside. I loved the enthusiasm of the early years with its earnest questioning like, 'Rev (the name they called their chaplain) – How did the blind man know it was Jesus when he couldn't see?' And I still laugh at the memory of the kindergarten girls in the middle of their first chapel service telling me that the ribbon I had wrapped around them to demonstrate the fold in which they were held by the shepherd of the sheep 'smelt like fish bait'. It did too!

I loved the experience of the middle years when students sat back in their chairs in the chapel and challenged me through their body language to do or say something important enough to gain their attention at all. I found that, in the end, it was the stories of real and struggling life which connected with them – for a moment! Then there were the marvellous times when students reminded me that once, when I was young, I had an immeasurable hope that things could be changed and an indestructible passion for justice, simply because I believed it should be.

In the middle of my time with the school, we had a funeral for the mother of two of the young students and it was an honour and privilege (as well as a great grief) to walk with them, their father and friends into the valley of death.

I will never forget the sound of the girls' voices singing what seemed to be their favourite hymn, 'Come as you are, that's how I want you' (Deirdre Brown). It moved me to tears to be reminded that from our earliest years we need the assurance that God really does love us 'just as we are' and convinced me again that this is the primary gospel message for the church to carry into the world.

So, thanks to all the students and staff and parents of MLC who gave me this opportunity and challenge.

Dorothy McRae-McMahon

USING THESE LITURGIES

Obviously, people who use these liturgies will take account of their own context and the way their people use liturgical material, just as I did in bringing these prayers together. Obviously, too, the recommended age group for each liturgy is just a guide. Many of them can cross age barriers and much depends on the life and worship experience of the young people.

All of these liturgies would benefit by the inclusion of music. I have left it for the users to decide what music they will add and where it should be placed. Music is a very cultural thing, even in the church these days. There are now very few 'well-known hymns' and sung responses! You will know best what music resonates with the souls of the young people you are serving.

I have not included an offering in the services because you will need to decide when that is appropriate. If it is appropriate, I would put it before the Prayers of Intercession. The headings for the elements in the service change with the recommended age groups so that children gradually realise that, for example, the Prayer of Confession is us saying we are sorry to God. You may prefer to move the Prayer of Confession to a less prominent place in the liturgy – as a sort of prelude to the Prayers of Intercession.

At the beginning of each liturgy, I have noted the main resources which would be needed for symbolic images or acts which are already written into the liturgy. I always assume that people add their own ideas about preparing the environment for liturgical events – that they will bring in their own cloths, candles, crosses, banners, contextual images or symbols, or anything else that might enhance the moment. I have just given some possible ideas which seemed to work with some young people. My suggestion, from hard experience, is that you keep it simple for maximum effect.

I have given the Bible readings which I was using to create the theme of each service. You will find that you can use others around the same theme. There are two services around the readings relating to the 'Woman at the well' and the 'Temptations of Jesus' – one for younger children and one for young people.

The concept of a book of liturgy is that it will give ideas to people, that they will adapt prayers and symbols for their own context. Good contemporary liturgy is an evolving event, made in spirit and in truth for each people and each place. So, feel free to take what I am offering and make it your own.

FOR FIVE TO SEVEN YEAR-OLDS

Suitable for 5–7 year-olds

WHAT IS PRAYER?

For this service, you will need:
A cross
A large candle
A piece of thick cord – long enough for each child to hang on to and to circle to reach to the table

GREETING

It is very good to be here together.
God is here with us, even if we can't see God.
God is like air around us.
Let us sit very still and feel the air
and imagine that God might be in the air near to us.

A silence is kept.

CROSS AND CANDLE

Today we will put on the table two things that remind us of Jesus.
The first is a cross.
This reminds us of the story of how Jesus lived with people.
The cross is placed on the table.
The second is a candle that you may help me light.
The candle is lit.
The candle reminds us that the way Jesus lived brings a light
that helps us see things better and understand them.
It also reminds us that Jesus warms us with love and care.

READING

Matthew 14:22-23

REFLECTION

This is a very, very small story in the Bible about Jesus going off by himself to pray.

What do you think that prayer is?

Children respond.

I am going to pass this strong cord around and I want each of you to hold onto it.

Then I am going to take the cord right up to the cross and candle that remind us of Jesus and God.

I think prayer is a bit like this. I have love inside myself and so do you. When we pray together, all that love is joined together as though we have a cord of love stretching between us all and making a circle of love around us. In the middle of that circle is the love of God. That love is bigger than all our love put together and it is joined with our love. When you put all that love together, good things happen. People feel cared for and comforted and that makes a big difference to them.

Sometimes in our prayers we tell God that we are sorry about something. Then God can help us feel that we are still loved. Mostly we pray for other people who need love and help, and we pray that we will know how best to care for them as well as God loving them. Prayer is really like talking to God and being part of God's loving of all people. Can you imagine yourself being in the middle of all that love and how good it would be?

Let us hold the cord and, as we say some prayers, imagine that you are joined together with all the other children and with God:

WE ARE SORRY

Dear God, we are sorry that we are not always good.
Sometimes we wish we had not done things or said things.
Sometimes we wish that we had cared more for other people.
Let us sit quietly and feel how we are all like that sometimes.

I am like that even as a grown-up.

A silence is kept.

Now let us imagine that God has heard what we say
and still loves us a lot and understands things.
Imagine that God's love is flowing down the cord into your hands
and God is saying:
I still love you, even though you are not good all the time.
Just start again as my special children.
Let's see if we can feel that.

A silence is kept.

WE PRAY FOR OTHERS

Now let us say another sort of prayer.
Let us think of people who need love,
who are sad,
or need food or safety or other help.
Can you think of anyone who is like that?

The children share.

Let us ask God to help those people.
Now imagine that there is lots of love
going right around the circle of the cord
so that our love for those people is made even stronger
because God's love is joined with it.

A silence is kept.

Thank you, God, for prayer
and for listening to us.

Amen.

Amen means 'So be it'.
It is a way of saying 'This is our prayer too'.
You can say 'Amen' after me,
because it is your prayer as well as mine.

The children say:

Amen.

Now we will put the cord on the table to remind us of prayer.

The cord is gathered up.

BLESSING

This is another sort of prayer, which is my prayer for you.
You can say 'Amen' after me at the end.
Go as the loved children of God.
And may you feel that love every day
like the sun on your faces
and be held safe in the hands of God.
Amen.

Amen.

GOD LOVES US

If the children are mostly five year-olds, they will obviously not read the responses. They can say things after you or simply listen. They often like to say the Amen after you. It is good to give an explanation of forgiveness. Perhaps something like: 'Forgiveness means that when we say we are sorry, God still loves us and is still our best friend'.

For this service, you will need:
Several small flat baskets
Grass or straw to form the nest (you could also use shredded paper)
Some small toy birds (you can usually find them in craft shops)
If you can't find the birds, pictures of birds would do
Some soft feathers (also often found in craft shops)

CALL TO WORSHIP

God loves every little bird,
and God loves us.
God loves trees and flowers and all that grows,
and God loves us.
God loves all the people in the world,
and God loves us.
Let us worship God!

WE ARE SORRY

We are sorry, dear God,
when we are not as loving as you are to us.
It is a bit hard to love everybody
and sometimes we would rather
just love our special friends.
We are sorry if we talk about other people unkindly.
Please forgive us, loving God.

Amen.

ASSURANCE OF FORGIVENESS

Forgiveness means that God still loves us.
God always forgives us when we are sorry.
We are forgiven, and we say thank you to God.

READING

Psalm 84:3-4
'Even the sparrow finds a home.'
or
Luke 12:24-28
'Consider the ravens; they neither sow nor reap,
they have neither storehouse nor barn, and yet God feeds them.'

REFLECTION

Most of us love little birds (*show the birds*). God loves us and little birds and everybody. Jesus told stories of the God who notices what happens to little birds and also what happens to us.

There is also a story about God being like a mother hen covering her chickens with her wings. This is the way God cares for us – like a mother hen covering us with her wings and keeping us loved and safe.

MAKING A NEST

Let us imagine that we are like little birds whom God loves. We could make a nest. Some children can come and put bits of grass, straw or paper in the basket to form the nest.

The children do so.

Now some others can cover this with feathers to keep the little birds cosy and warm, just like the mother bird does.

Other children do so.

Now some of you can put a little bird in the nest.

Choose children who have not had a turn.

God is just like a mother bird covering us with warm feathers when we feel a bit lonely or scared or sad.

PRAYERS FOR OTHERS

Who would we like to pray for today?

The children share and the prayers are said.

Dear God, we know that you see everyone who is hurt or lonely or sick today,
people whom we never notice or who are far away.
We pray that they will feel like small birds in a warm nest,
wrapped around with your loving care.
We pray for all the children and teachers here,
and we pray in the name of Jesus.

Amen.

BLESSING

Go out as the loved children of God.
And may every bird sing with the joy of God,
every tree wave in delight because Jesus is near,
and every friend be, to you, the love of the Holy Spirit.

Amen.

Suitable for 5–11 year-olds

BRINGING OUR GIFTS

For this service, you will need:
A candle
A long cloth – preferably green
Baskets with small pieces of paper and pencils

CALL TO WORSHIP

God loves us and gives us many gifts:
things we need for our life,
love that is always around us
and kindness when we are sad.
God loves us and gives us many gifts:
laughter and fun,
music and flowers,
friends and family to be with us as we go.
God is good to us every day.

LIGHTING THE CANDLE

Let us light this candle to remind us
that God is full of light and warmth.

The candle is lit.

WE ARE SORRY

Dear God, we are sorry
when we are given more things than we need,
but we don't share them with other people
who need them because they don't have enough.
We are sorry for that, dear God,
and ask you to forgive us.

Amen.

GOD FORGIVES US

Jesus knows that we don't always do the right thing
and still loves us,
especially when we say we are sorry.
We are forgiven.

Thanks be to God.

READING

John 6:1-21

REFLECTION

This is a story of Jesus seeing all the people who had come to hear him. They
had walked a long way and there were no shops where they could buy their
meal. Jesus was wondering what to do when a little boy came and gave him
a gift of bread and fish. It wasn't much. It was probably the little boy's lunch,
but Jesus was very grateful to receive it and in some special way managed to
make it enough to give all the people something to eat. They even had lots of
food left over.

When we hear stories like this, they are beautiful stories to think about.
What does the story really mean?
Maybe it means that, even though we are small and don't feel very important,
we can give gifts to Jesus to help change things and make the world a more
loving place.

Of course, we couldn't bring our lunch to Jesus these days because we can't
see him. But sometimes we can share what food we have with other people
or give a gift of money that helps buy food for them.

Sometimes it's not food we share but just things about ourselves. If you think
about yourself, what do you like best about yourself? What do you think you
give to other people just because they know you? When I think of myself, I
think I am usually a rather kind person. I think I could bring my kindness and
give it to Jesus.

Because I can't see him these days, I know he would like me to give my
kindness to other people.

Maybe you are brave, or you can think well, or you are good at making things or helping clean up, or perhaps you are good at being friends with people? What is good about you, do you think?

Whatever you think you are good at is the gift you bring to Jesus by being yourself and offering the thing you are good at to others – like the boy who gave his bread and fish to Jesus. He was good at sharing, wasn't he?

BRINGING OUR GIFTS

Let us imagine that this long cloth is like a picnic cloth.
It is spread out, ready for all the good things to be put on it.

The cloth is spread down among the children.

In these baskets are pieces of paper and pencils. If you like, you can take some paper and a pencil and think of what you like best about yourself. Write it on the paper or do a little drawing of yourself on the paper and just think what you are good at. When you are ready, put it in one of the baskets which we will pass around. Then we will put the baskets on the cloth. Of course, there will not be food in these picnic baskets but lots of other good things to share with people.

The baskets are passed around and the children place their gifts in the baskets.

PRAYER OF THANKS
AND PRAYER FOR OTHERS

Dear God, we thank you that you made us different from one another,
with all sorts of things to give to other people.
We thank you that some of us are strong, some of us are brave,
some do kind things,
and some of us share what we have that day.
We thank you, O God,
that some of us listen carefully when people need someone to talk to,
some of us can sing well, while others are good at drawing.

We thank you for the times when someone gives a gift to us
and for the times when we can give a gift ourselves.
We pray for people who need gifts from others but don't get them
because no-one knows they need them,
or they are lonely or far away from other people.
We will think for a moment about people like that.

A silence is kept.

We pray for people who feel too shy to ask for help,
who are embarrassed or think no-one would care for them.
We pray for people who live in countries
where almost everyone needs gifts
because they are poor or there has been a war.
Let us think about people like that.

A silence is kept.

And now, dear God, we pray that you will be with us all,
helping us to give kindly to others
and to ask when we need care from them.
We pray because we know that Jesus loves us.

Amen.

SENDING OUT AND BLESSING

Let us go as people who hold lots of good things to give to others,
and may we feel the hands of Jesus outstretched to receive what we offer,
the Holy Spirit singing in joy when we are loving,
and God who is our loving Parent going with us on the way.

Amen.

GOD FINDS US

For this service, you will need:

A large candle
Two small fluffy lambs which are 'hidden' behind something on the communion table
A roll of ribbon long enough to go around the whole group of children

CALL TO WORSHIP

I am going to talk about God, like a sort of little poem.
People sometimes do that when they come to church.
I am going to say things about God loving us.
When you hear me say:
'God finds us', you could say it after me.
Let's try that.
God finds us.
God finds us.

Now I am going to say some words in between,
but as soon as you hear me say
'God finds us', you can say that too.

God looks for every little lamb or lost bird.
God finds us.
God finds us.

God watches to see if anyone is lonely.
God finds us.
God finds us.

God sees and loves everyone in the world.
God finds us.
God finds us.

WE ARE SORRY

When I have finished this prayer when we talk to God,
I will say 'Amen'.
You can say 'Amen' after me.
That means that this is not just my prayer, it is your prayer too.

We are sorry, dear God,
when we are not very kind to other people.
Sometimes we don't know what to say to people
or feel a bit too busy doing what we are doing.
Please forgive us, loving God.
Amen.
Amen.

GOD FORGIVES US

God always forgives us when we are sorry.
God finds us and loves us,
even when we are a bit worried about ourselves.
We are forgiven.
Amen.
Amen.

READING

Matthew 18:12-14

SONG

REFLECTION

Jesus told this story about how God really loves people, especially people
who feel a bit lost. In the place where Jesus lived, because it was often very
cold and there were wolves around, every night the shepherd (the one who
looked after sheep) would gather all the sheep into a sheepfold. This was a
sort of small paddock with a fence and a gate. The sheep would all huddle
together to keep warm and the fence would keep them safe from the wolves.
Sometimes, if there were just a few sheep, they were put into a big barn or
even taken inside the house with the people. Jesus was saying that God is
like the shepherd who looks after the sheep.

I am going to pretend that I am the shepherd and you are my sheep. This ribbon that I am going to place around you is a pretend fence. So, here you are all together and feeling safe because you are warm and inside the fence.

The ribbon is placed around the children.

In the story that Jesus told, there was one little lamb who was lost. This little lamb had probably wandered off during the day and couldn't find the way back to the other sheep. Wouldn't that be awful if you were like this little lamb all by yourself out in the cold? Jesus said that God wouldn't give up until he found that little lamb and brought the lamb back with the others safe, into the fold.

See if you can see any little lost lamb around here. If you look hard, you might see the lost lamb. Do you think this is a little girl lamb or a little boy lamb? Maybe there could be two who are lost? Let's see if we can find another.

The children look and point to the lamb/s.

There they are, and we will hold them to keep them warm and put them with everyone in the safe place.

The lambs are placed inside the ribbon.

God is like that. When we feel lost or lonely or sad, even though we can't see God, God is there with us loving us. So if you ever feel like that, just stop and feel the air around you as though God is in the air and keeping you warm and loved.

PRAYERS FOR OTHERS AND OURSELVES
Who would we like to pray for today?

The children share and the prayers are said.

Dear God, send your love to all these people who need you.
Be with any little children who feel as though they are not loved enough or haven't warm clothes or houses in the winter.
Be with any of us who are a bit scared or lonely.
We are glad that you love us all.
Amen.
Amen.

SENDING OUT AND BLESSING

Go out as the loved children of God.
And may every little lamb remind you of the kindness of God,
every warm sunny day remind you of the God who wants us all to feel warm,
and everyone you meet keep you safe.
Amen.
Amen.

FOR EIGHT TO TWELVE YEAR-OLDS

Suitable for 8–12 year-olds

ANYONE CAN BE THE ONE

For this service, you will need:
A large candle placed on the table
A large flat basket or tray of mixed flowers and leaves

GREETING

Christ be with you.
And also with you.

CALL TO WORSHIP

God surprises us,
surprises us in other people,
and surprises us in ourselves.
God loves to surprise us with good things,
with new ways of seeing each other
and with little gifts of love.
Let us be thankful for God.

The candle is lit.

WE ARE SORRY

We are sorry, loving Jesus,
when we don't want to hear good things
about people we don't like much.
We are sorry when we think we know
everything about everybody
and would rather not know anything new.
We are sorry about that, loving Jesus.
We are sorry and would like to change.

Amen.

GOD FORGIVES US

Jesus knows that we are sorry and still loves us.
Jesus is busy looking for all sorts of good things in us,
even when we are not the people we would want to be.
We are forgiven.

Thanks be to God.

READING

Mark 6:1-13

REFLECTION

This story about Jesus shows us that we can often think we know someone and then they surprise us.

The people who were listening to Jesus didn't want to hear what he was saying because they thought he wasn't important enough to say anything special. His father was a carpenter and they thought that meant that he wouldn't have anything to say that they should listen to. They saw carpenters and their families as very ordinary – people who should just stick to working with wood rather than telling other people anything.

Do you think we ever see people like that today? I think I sometimes do. I think I would be surprised if the rubbish man went on TV and told us what sort of country we should be.

When I was at school, I must say I had my own special friends and we didn't like some other girls and boys in our school. We used to talk about them during lunch or break time. We rather liked talking about them actually. We sometimes used to notice girls or boys who didn't have quite the right school uniform and we thought they didn't come from as good a home as we had. Sometimes I was the one who looked a bit different because my mum and dad didn't have enough money and I felt as though people were talking about me.

Just sometimes, I used to notice that one of those girls or boys, whom my friends and I didn't like, did or said something good. I didn't say anything to my friends because they mightn't like me saying that about someone we didn't like. I just kept it to myself and thought about it.

Then there were the times when I met someone again after a long time and was really surprised about how much better I liked them than I had before. I would think to myself that they must have changed a lot as they grew a bit older. I didn't often think that maybe I was the one who had changed and was now seeing that person differently.

I think God really likes surprising us about other people. It helps us not to be so sure that we really know people – not to make up our minds too quickly. It also teaches us that, even if people are not so nice some of the time, they might be very kind or wise at another time. We are all a bit like that, aren't we? Then God loves to show us that the people whom we thought were very ordinary and unimportant can sometimes be very special.

Any of us could be the one to give a gift to others – gifts of being wise, of being loving, of being brave or telling the truth.

PEOPLE ARE SPECIAL IN DIFFERENT WAYS

Here is a beautiful basket of flowers and leaves – all sorts of flowers and leaves.

When you look at them you might think you like one best.

Then you might see another which is different but also beautiful.

There might be one which looks a bit droopy and ordinary because it isn't getting enough water. Then you give it some water and it suddenly looks quite different.

Or maybe it is just a little tight bud and later becomes a splendid colourful flower. Or perhaps it started out as a very ordinary leaf and then changes colour.

People are rather like that, aren't they?

Today, I would like you to choose any one of these flowers or leaves and decide who it reminds you of – it might be your best friend, or yourself, or someone whom you haven't much liked before but would like to see differently.

Choose your flower or leaf from the basket as I pass it around, hold it in your hand and think about it, then when you are ready come and place it near the candle which is like the warm light of Jesus.

The children do so.

PRAYERS FOR OTHERS AND OURSELVES

Dear God, we pray for any children who feel that they are different
and that other people don't like them.
We pray for children who think that
they could never do anything good or helpful for everyone.
We pray for people all over the world
who think that they are not important to you or to us
because they are ill or not very clever or are poor.
We will be very quiet and think about them, loving Jesus.
You understand all about us because you are one of us as well as God.
We are sending our loving thoughts to all these people as we pray to you.

A silence is kept.

Then we pray for ourselves,
that we will be children who are kindly
and who find all sorts of good things in many people around us.
Care for any of us who feel lonely and unloved, O God,
and be with us as we live and play together.

Amen.

SENDING OUT AND BLESSING

Let us go and look for God's surprises all over the place
and in all sorts of people.
And may Jesus help us to see,
the Holy Spirit give us ears to listen for good things,
and God our loving Parent love all of us.

Amen.

Suitable for 8–12 year-olds

BEING BORN AGAIN

For this service, you will need:
If possible, three dolls – black, white and Asian (Asian dolls can often be found in the 'Chinatown' area in large cities)
Seeds and pictures of the plant that they represent
A few buds – some that the children will recognise and some they will not

CALL TO WORSHIP

God who creates in love
and watches over all our beginnings,
like a mother and a father,

we worship you.

God who is excited when we grow and learn,
just as our parents and teachers are excited,

we worship you.

God who encourages us and cares for us,
like our best friend,

we worship you today.

WE ARE SORRY

Dear God, we are sorry when we don't give other people
a chance to be a bit different
because we think it is better that they are like us.

Silence.

Forgive us, loving God.

Amen.

ASSURANCE OF FORGIVENESS

God forgives us and makes every day
a new day for starting again.
We are forgiven!

Thanks be to God.

READING

John 3:1-17
In this is the word of our God.

Thanks be to God.

REFLECTION

Remembering when we were born…

· When you are born, your mother and father have been part of beginning somebody new.

· You live within your mother and she cares for you and feeds you.

· Then she works very hard and often goes through some pain in bringing you to birth.

· Until you arrive, she doesn't know what you will look like or what sort of person you will be. (Show different dolls, black, white and Asian.)

· Being born again is rather like that.

· You often start thinking about being someone new, someone different.

· You learn and grow and wait.

· Sometimes you do some hard work and life is a bit tough.

· Then, if you ask God to help with all this, you often find that you end up being a different sort of person which God helps you to be – perhaps even different from the person you thought you would like to be.

SEEDS AND BUDS

It is all a bit like these seeds and buds.
If I show them to you, it would be rather hard for you to tell me what they
would look like when they grow.
I will show you a seed and then a picture (or example) of the plant they
become.
Can you guess what this bud will open into?
Our lives are often like that.

PRAYERS FOR OTHERS AND OURSELVES

Dear God, we pray for people
who would really like to start something new
or be someone different,
but are afraid to begin.

We are quiet.

We pray for people who find it hard to do anything much
because they have lost their homes in war,
or because someone they love has died.
We pray for children who spend their lives
looking for food and water
rather than having the chance to do interesting things.
We pray that you will help and comfort them, O God,
and that we will be able to share in caring for them.

We are quiet.

And then we pray for ourselves today, O God.

**Hold us in your loving hands,
keep us ready to grow and learn.
We pray this in the name of Jesus.
Amen.**

SENDING OUT AND BLESSING

Go as the children of God.
and may the day be warm around you like the love of God,
may everywhere you go be a place of gentle care like Jesus your friend
and may the Holy Spirit be very near to you.

Amen.

Suitable for 8–12 year-olds

GIVING CHANGES PEOPLE
For this service, you will need:
A large candle on the table
Numbers of smaller candles beside the larger candle, on a plate/s
Tapers for lighting the small candles

GREETING

Christ be with you.
And also with you.

CALL TO WORSHIP

You are a God who gives to us,

and we thank you.

You are a God who understands us,

and we thank you.

You are a God who always loves us,

and we have come to worship you today.

LIGHTING THE CANDLE

Let us light this candle that reminds us of the warmth of the love of God.

The candle is lit.

WE ARE SORRY

Dear God, we are sorry
that we sometimes don't see the good in other people
and wouldn't expect them to give us anything.
You understand when this happens,
because you know what people are like.

Amen.

GOD FORGIVES US

God always forgives us when we are sorry.
Jesus knows what it is like to be a person like us.
We are forgiven.

Thanks be to God!

READING

John 4:5-15
In this is the word of our God for us.

Thanks be to God.

REFLECTION

· The Samaritans were people whom the Jews didn't like. They didn't talk to them or make friends with them – they kept as far away from them as possible.

· Most Jewish men didn't talk to women, other than those they knew. They also didn't think women had much to offer to them.

· Jesus sits down and talks to a Samaritan woman and one who was even rejected by her own people because of the way she lived her life.

· He asks something of her and gives something to her.

· She is surprised by his respect for her and so are the friends of Jesus.

· Jesus shows us that God sees more in us than others do and, no matter who we are, gives us gifts.

· That woman was probably changed. She would see herself as a person who was honoured by Jesus and given a new gift of life.

· We can do that for each other.

PRAYERS FOR OTHERS AND OURSELVES

Who do you think needs more love in our world?
If you can think of someone or some people, come and light a little candle on the table from the candle which we lit to remind us of the love of God.

This little candle will be a sign that we would like these people to be warmed by love –
our love and the love of God.

The children do so.

We pray for all these people, O God,
and all the other people whom we do not know who are sad and lonely.
We pray for all the children here.
May they always feel loved and wanted,
and may we all find friends.
Care for us today, Jesus Christ.
We pray in your name.

Amen.

BLESSING

Go out into the world as God's loved children.
And may God hold you safely like a mother,
Jesus Christ take your hand like a brother,
and the Holy Spirit cover you with warm wings.

Amen.

GOING DOWN DEEPLY

For this service, you will need:
A long coloured cloth
A small doll
A large candle

GREETING

Christ be with you.
And also with you.

CALL TO WORSHIP

God lives deep down in our lives.

God is good.

God goes with us into our deep, deep thinking.

God is love.

God is not afraid of quiet, deep places.

God is always there.
Let us worship God.

WE ARE SORRY

We are sorry, loving God, that we sometimes fail you.
We try quite hard but still we don't always do the right thing
and we are not always the people you would like us to be.
We are sorry, loving God, and we ask you to forgive us.

Amen.

GOD FORGIVES US

The good news is that God does forgive us,
because Jesus was once a child like us
and knows what our life is like.
We are forgiven!

Thanks be to God.

THE READING

Matthew 4:1-11
In this is the word for us.

Thanks be to God.

REFLECTION

You might have heard in another service the story of Jesus being tempted. Possibly the person who was talking about that story told you how Jesus was just like us and sometimes felt like doing things he should not do – so he understands when that happens to us.

The Bible is an interesting book because almost every story has lots of different meanings. So, here is another meaning for the story about Jesus stopping and spending time by himself in the wilderness.

- Jesus was doing a good thing because instead of rushing around all the time doing things and fixing things, he knew that every now and then he should stop and think deeply about his life and where he was going.

- I am going to tell you a story about going deep down in the water and it will remind you of Jesus bravely thinking about his life – which can be a bit scary at times.

- Once upon a time when I was a little girl, about as old as you are, I was very shy. I used to watch other girls and boys doing all sorts of things and wish I was as brave as they were. Sometimes they did things like diving off the edge of the swimming pool. It looked such fun and they all splashed and laughed but I was too scared and used to climb down the steps and just slip into the water. Then one day I was standing watching and my good friend threw a ball into the water and said, 'Go, Dorothy! Throw it back to me!' I shut my eyes and jumped into the water and swam as fast as I could to get the ball. It was great fun and I felt as though I was as brave as everyone else. Later on, I still felt a bit scared, but I knew I had done it once and could be brave enough to do it again.

- Sometimes I find it a bit scary to stop and think about myself because I get a bit worried about next week or next year, or I think of special things I could be and remember I am mostly not very special.

- Lots of times as I have grown older, I have stopped and thought about how I am not very brave about things. I have not said what I really wanted to say in case people would not be my friends, or I have not done what I should do because people might not be nice to me. Sometimes I have done things that I wish I hadn't done and I find it hard to think about that because I am worried about it.

This story reminds us that God loves us as we stop and go a bit deeper into things. Sometimes that feels like jumping off the edge into deep water, but when we do, it is good after all.

LIGHTING THE CANDLE

This cloth is like the journey of our life.

The cloth is placed running down from a table or pedestal onto the floor.

When we stop and think, sometimes it is like going down deep all by ourselves.

The small doll is placed at the bottom of the cloth.

But God is always down deep in our lives and never leaves alone. God is like this candle – warm and giving light beside us.

The candle is placed near to the doll and lit.

PRAYERS FOR OTHERS AND OURSELVES

Dear God, we pray for lonely people,
for children who feel afraid and lost
without enough people to talk to and to have as friends.
We pray that you will be with them
and that we will be with them as much as we can.
Let us think about that by ourselves for a moment.

Silent prayer

We pray also for ourselves,
when we are rushed and bothered,
when it seems hard to stop and be quiet
and to think deeply and to feel your love for us.
Hold us in your care, we pray, in Jesus' name.

Amen.

BLESSING

Go out as brave people today, people who go deeply into life.
And may you find God at the bottom of every deep place,
Jesus take your hand as you stand there,
and the Holy Spirit wrap you round with love.
Amen.

JESUS CARES FOR US WHEN WE ARE SAD

This service can be used simply as part of the lectionary themes. It can also be used if there has been a death among young children. It was originally used when the mother of two young girls in a school had died.

For this service, you will need:
Felt pens – enough to share.
Strips of coloured ribbon about 3 cm wide and 50 cm long
A basket for the ribbons

GREETING

Christ be with you.
And also with you.

CALL TO WORSHIP

When we feel lost and cold inside,

God loves us.

When people we love die or leave us,

God loves and cares for us.

When the world around us seems full of sadness,

God loves us all.
Let us worship God.

WE ARE SORRY

Dear God, sometimes we forget to ask you to help us
when we are sad or afraid.
We try to cope all by ourselves
when you are just waiting to care for us.

Silent reflection

Sometimes we don't know what to say

when other people are sad,
so we keep way from them
in case we get upset, or they get upset.

Silent reflection

Forgive us, loving Jesus,
and remind us that you are always with us.

Amen.

WE ARE FORGIVEN

Jesus said that God is always with us,
when we are happy and when we are sad.
This is God's promise to us.
We are forgiven.

Thanks be to God.

READING

John 11:1-6, 17-45

In this is the word of the Lord.
Thanks be to God.

REFLECTION

We all know that people die. Sometimes they die because they are very old,
sometimes because they are very sick or sometimes because they have an
accident. We are always sad when people die because we will miss them. We
cry, just like Jesus cried when his friend Lazarus died. The story tells us that
Jesus made Lazarus alive again, but we have never seen that happen today.
It would sometimes be good if we could have people made alive again, but
that doesn't seem to happen. What we do know is that God cares for us when
we are sad and that we can care for each other and that helps us to feel
better after a while.

It is often hard to know what to say to people who are very sad because
we are a bit scared of making them cry and then we mightn't know what
to do. Sometimes we just keep away from them in case they are upset, and

they feel every lonely. It is really best to treat them just like we always do. Sometimes we might feel like asking them if they want to talk about being sad. Sometimes they do and sometimes they don't. That is OK.

If they cry, we don't need to worry. We just hold their hand or give them a hug. Crying often helps when we are sad. Sometimes we cry a bit with them. If it feels as though things are a bit too tough and they can't stop crying, it is best just quietly to get a grown-up to help comfort them.

The main thing is still to be good friends with people who are sad. After a while, people do feel better and they just think very lovingly of the person who has died, like a very special memory.

PRAYERS FOR OTHERS AND OURSELVES

Dear God, we pray today for all people who have lost someone they loved because they died in a war
or died because they didn't have enough to eat
or because they were ill or had an accident.
We pray that you will be very close to them today
and care for them. Especially we pray for…

Silent prayer

Loving Jesus, we pray for ourselves,
all the children here and our teachers and parents.
You know best if any of us is sad or feeling that life is hard for us.

Be our friend, Jesus Christ, and weep with us.
Comfort those who need comfort
and give new life among us.

Amen.

(Choose one of the following options.)

IF SOMEONE HAS DIED

Prayer is like placing a ribbon of love around people with a very loving God in the centre who makes our love even stronger. We are going to give each of you a ribbon and a pen.

Write your name on the ribbon and we will put all the ribbons together in a beautiful bunch tied with a bow. We will give the ribbons to *(Names)* who are sad. They will be having a special service called a funeral to say a special goodbye to *(Name)*, and we will give the ribbons to them then so that they know that all their friends are praying for them and loving them.

The children write on the ribbons and the ribbons are collected in a basket.

IF THERE HAVE BEEN NO DEATHS CONNECTED DIRECTLY WITH THE CHILDREN

You can do the above, but think of some group of people or a person who is sad and needs prayers, and adapt the service.

SENDING OUT AND BLESSING

Go into this week as God's loved children.
And may the whole earth be filled with songs of hope,
the sun and the moon shine with the love of God,
and our lives be new every day.

Amen.

ROLL OUT THE RED CARPET

For this service, you will need:
A long red cloth – long enough to roll out down the aisle
A basket containing small green branches

GREETING

Christ be with you.
And also with you.

CALL TO WORSHIP

Jesus comes in the name of our God!
Praise to the Christ, the brave one!

Praise be to God.

Jesus rides through the people
in love and courage,
never turning away in fear.

Praise be to Jesus Christ!
Let us worship God.

ROLLING OUT THE RED CARPET

As the people of old spread palm leaves for Jesus,
we will roll out a red carpet for good to walk through our life.

The 'carpet' is rolled out.

WE ARE SORRY

Brave Jesus,
sometimes we are not very brave
in supporting people who need us.
We worry about what other people think

and sometimes we don't care very much
about how others are feeling.
Dear Jesus, you love us as ordinary children,
forgive us as you did your friends so long ago.

Amen.

WE ARE FORGIVEN

Jesus never forgets us.
We are remembered every day of our lives.
We are loved and forgiven.
Thanks be to God.

READING

Matthew 21:1-11
In this is the word of the Lord.
Thanks be to God.

REFLECTION

· Jesus was bravely going down the road to Jerusalem where he knew
there were people who might wish to harm him and who did not like
what he was doing and saying. They were the same leaders who often
made life hard and unjust for ordinary people.

· He was riding on a donkey, rather than a horse, because people who rode
on horses looked as though they were coming to fight others – people
who were coming as part of a war. A donkey was an ordinary everyday
animal which people used for travel.

· Lots of people loved Jesus by this time and they gathered along the road
to cheer him on and they waved palm branches and placed them on the
road like the red carpet that we lay out for important people to walk on
when there is a special occasion of welcome.

· We could imagine that Jesus on Palm Sunday is like goodness and
kindness and justice being given a welcome into our life.

· Sometimes when people try to bring in goodness, they have a hard and
suffering time, as Jesus did later, but on this day we celebrate that the
coming of goodness in Jesus was cheered by the crowds.

PRAYERS FOR OTHERS AND OURSELVES

Loving Jesus, we remember how, a long time ago,
the people stood by the road and welcomed you.
We pray that we too will welcome you,
that we will be people who welcome
goodness and kindness when we see it.

We pray for all people who need our love today:
people who feel that nobody knows
how hard their life is,
people who struggle for enough to live,
and people who are ill or sad.

Let us place branches beside the cloth
as we remember some of the people and places
who need our care and the love of Jesus today;
let us also remember all those people who are trying to help.
These branches could be a sort of welcome
to all people who need a special place in our life.
This could be a place where we cheer them on.

The branches are placed on the red cloth.

Who do you think those people are?

The children call out the names of people; candles are lit and placed on the cloth.

Bless us all, Jesus Christ,
especially any children who feel a need for support
or who are lonely among us.

**We pray for our parents and teachers
as they try to roll out red carpets
that will guide us towards learning and growing.
We pray in your name.**

Amen.

SENDING OUT AND BLESSING

We are the ones who cheer goodness on the way.
Go into the world in hope and celebration.
And may Jesus feel as close as our best friend,
the love of God be near to us every day,
and the Holy Spirit take us by the hand.

Amen.

SHARING A MEAL

For this service, you will need:
A large loaf of bread
A chalice

THE CALL TO WORSHIP

As we love one another,

God is with us.

As we share food with one another,

God is with us.

Loving and sharing are the signs of God.

Let us worship God.

WE ARE SORRY

Dear God, we are sorry when we eat lots of food
without thinking of people who have little to eat,
or when we would rather not share things.
Forgive us, loving Jesus.

Amen.

GOD FORGIVES US

Jesus knows what it is like to be a child like us
and loves us, even when we make mistakes.
We are forgiven.

Thanks be to God.

READING

Luke 24:13-35

In this is the word of the Lord.

Thanks be to God.

REFLECTION

- The disciples on the road to Emmaus are worried and puzzled.

- Jesus often comes to be with us as we feel like that, and sometimes this helps us to see things more clearly and helpfully.

- Sometimes this happens when we are sharing time with friends, perhaps having a meal together.

- This meal that Jesus had with his Emmaus friends reminds us of the meal that Christians call Holy Communion or the Eucharist when we share bread and wine and believe that Jesus is with us in that meal (*showing bread and chalice*).

- We will share a loaf of bread together today and remember those special meals.

SHARING OF BREAD

A loaf of bread is broken into large pieces and the children give each other a piece of bread and eat it together as they are encouraged to think of the Bible story.

PRAYERS FOR OTHERS

Loving God,
we pray for children all over the world who do not have enough.
We pray for children who do not have enough love,
or enough to eat,
and for children who are afraid
because they live in a place of war.
Especially, we think today of the children
who live where you used to live as a child –
the Palestinian and Israeli children.

Please help peace to come to their country, O God.
We also pray for ourselves,
for all the children here and our teachers,
and for our parents at home.

**Make us more loving every day,
ready to share things with each other
and to gather lonely people into our groups.**

Amen.

SENDING OUT AND BLESSING

Go into this week, as the loved children of God,
precious to each other and to many people.
And may the God of grace watch over you,
Jesus Christ be your friend in every moment,
and the Holy Spirit hold you close.

Amen.

FOR TWELVE TO EIGHTEEN YEAR-OLDS

Suitable for 11–14 year-olds

I SEE!

GREETING

Christ be with you.
And also with you.

CALL TO WORSHIP

God, who opens our eyes,
and brings miracles to humble people,

we have come to worship you.

God, who opens our eyes,
and startles us so that we see others
and the world in a different way,

we have come to worship you this day.

CONFESSION

Loving God, in a world where there is often suffering,
we sometimes find it hard to believe in miracles.
Sometimes it is even difficult to pray to you
in case we are disappointed.

Silent reflection

We also confess, O God, that we don't always see those
who are waiting for healing and support.

We are sorry about that and pray that you will open our eyes
to the needs of others.
Forgive us and give to us a new start.
We pray in your name.
Amen.

ASSURANCE OF FORGIVENESS

Jesus always hears our prayers
and comes close to us in love.
We are forgiven.

Thanks be to God.

READINGS

Psalm 23
In this is the word of the Lord.

Thanks be to God.

John 9:1-11

This is the gospel of Jesus Christ.

Praise to you, Lord Jesus Christ.

REFLECTION

• People have always tried to understand human suffering.

  Some people blame it on the person who is suffering – they must have done something wrong or haven't enough faith.

• Some people blame it on God.

  The blind man whom Jesus healed was almost certainly physically blind.

  I have seen real miracles of physical healing happen, but it is not always that way when we pray. I have often prayed and the miracle of healing doesn't happen in the way that I hoped.

• When we pray for a miracle, we need to give some thought to what prayer means or else we may become discouraged.

We ask God to help us.

We wait for the love of God in some form and look around to find it.
We cannot tell what that will be like.
It may indeed be actual physical healing.
It may be strength and courage or support from others
– a gathering of love around us.

If we could simply demand what we want in prayers, we would be God.

• Prayer is like the joining together of all our love with the love of God and many surprising gifts can come from that – things we may never have expected.

• Going back to the story – there are many ways of being blind.

Sometimes we can be blind in other ways – like not seeing other people clearly, or not seeing the truth clearly.

Praying to God can help us with that sort of blindness too.

PRAYERS FOR OTHERS AND OURSELVES

Loving Jesus, we will cover our eyes with our hands,
so that we may be still, and silent,
shutting out all the rushing moments of our lives,
so that we may see our lives and the lives of others more clearly.
Let us all cover our eyes.

A time of silence

And now, O God, we pray for those
who seem unimportant to most people,
waiting in hope for someone to see them and care for them.
We especially pray for all people who cannot see,
who need help and respect from us
as they bravely live their lives.

Silent reflection

Then we pray for ourselves
and for our teachers and our parents.

**May we all live together lovingly,
seeing each other as you see us with the eyes of love,
caring for others who need our support,
in the name of the Christ.**

Amen.

SENDING OUT AND BLESSING

Go out from this place
as those whose eyes have been opened
to new visions of the power and love of God.
And may Jesus stop and see us when we are in need,
the Holy Creator be our loving parent,
and the Spirit dance down the road ahead of us.

Amen.

Suitable for 11–14 year-olds

JESUS IS ALIVE!

For this service, you will need:
A large candle placed on the table with celebratory flowers around it
A cloth flowing from the candle across the table or down onto the floor
into the central aisle
Small candles and the means of lighting them

GREETING

Christ be with you.
And also with you.

CALL TO WORSHIP

Love is stronger than hate,
for Jesus Christ is risen.
Life is stronger than death,
for Jesus Christ is risen.
Come as you are,
for Jesus Christ is risen
and gathers us all into the love of God.
Let us worship God!

LIGHTING THE CANDLE

We will light this candle as a sign that Jesus Christ is alive
and spreading light into all the world.

The candle is lit.

WE ARE SORRY

Dear God, we are sorry that we sometimes find it hard to believe
that you love all people.
Sometimes, as we look at the world,

we find it hard to believe that you have risen
and that good is strong.

Forgive us when we feel like that.

Amen.

GOD FORGIVES US

Jesus comes to us again today,
deep within our hearts,
and brings love and kindness to us.
We are forgiven.

Thanks be to God.

READING

John 20:19-31
This is the gospel of Jesus Christ.

Praise to you, Lord Jesus Christ.

REFLECTION

We could say that we worship God because Jesus rose from the dead like a sort of magic person. It is a marvellous and mysterious thing that Jesus came to life.

However, the important thing is that we think about what this means.

What do you think it means?

I think it is a special sign to us that good is never defeated.

That is very hard to believe because it often seems like the bad wins, but the life of Jesus tells us that this will not be forever. It says to us that we are to look for all sorts of little signs that good is in the world, that Jesus is working away with us to change things into justice, peace and love.

Where have you seen that?

Where do you see kindness and brave people working for a better world?

This is where I see some of that:

I remember meeting a young woman from the Philippines at a time when people there were struggling for freedom and justice against their President, named President Marcos. She was only 21 years old and her name was Jessica Sales. She had just finished university and was working with the families of people who had been put in prison because they dared to speak out against President Marcos. We were at a conference together and she was speaking about her work. When she finished, she came and sat beside me and said, 'I think those words may cost me my life, Dorothy'. I didn't know what to say. Then she said, 'But I have to live'. I knew that she meant that she cared so much about her people and the struggle for justice that, even if she died, she would rather keep doing her work and speaking about it. She did die. When she returned home, she was arrested and tortured and killed. But somehow I knew that she was more alive than any of those who killed her and that her life would live on in the hearts of people when they were long forgotten.

Thankfully, most of us will never need to die in order to be truly alive. We will be the ones who do small, often unexpected and sometimes brave things that remind other people that good is still alive and that hopelessness, unkindness and all the things that take from life will never win in the end.

Maybe you can see signs that Jesus is alive and well among us in your friends. It is good to point to those things when we see them, and support and encourage them.

We can be part of that as we are a loving people. That is why we are called the body of Christ.

PRAYERS FOR OTHERS AND OURSELVES

Dear Jesus, who stood in kindness
among the early disciples,
as they looked and found the marks of pain and suffering
on your hands and in your side,
so we look for the marks of suffering in the world around us.
Let us say the names of the places where we see suffering
and light these small candles
as little symbols of the loving life of God
carried by Jesus Christ into the world.

The names are said and candles are lit and placed along the cloth.

We pray that you will care for all these people,

as you loved your first friends, loving Jesus.
Give them justice and peace,
and enough for their daily needs.
Help us to be your caring people in the world.
We pray for ourselves, our teachers and our parents.

**Help us to see the good in each other that comes from you
and help us to know the times when others need our love.**

Amen.

BLESSING

Go in peace because Jesus Christ is alive.
Go in hope because we are the loved children of God.
And may Jesus Christ be found among our friends,
God the loving Parent guide us on the way,
and the Holy Spirit fill us with joy.

Amen.

CELEBRATING THE BIBLE

For this service, you will need:
A large Bible
A long flowing cloth (suggest purple)
A candle
A bud
A small cross
A bowl of charcoal or a smaller red cloth
Lengths of wide coloured ribbon

GREETING

The peace of Christ be with you.
And also with you.

CALL TO WORSHIP

We are the people of the word, the Bible.
Here we read the wisdom of many centuries,
the stories of those who knew Jesus Christ
and the journeying of the people towards their God.
The Bible is carried in and placed on the holy table.
We are the people of the word, the Bible,
holding in our hands our sacred texts for life,
hope told in courage by prophets and in saints,
the Bible, a meeting place with our God.

The Bible is held high.

This is the Holy Bible of our faith.
We are the people of the word.
Let us worship our God.

A flowing cloth is spread from the Bible down the aisle towards the people.

CONFESSION

O God, we thank you that the people in the Bible
bring us the stories of their life.
We are glad that their lives are like ours.
They made their mistakes and were sorry.
They often found it hard to believe in you.
We are thankful that we can place our life stories beside theirs.

The Bible is carried and placed on the cloth in the centre of the people.

O God, even though we have the Bible to help us and advise us,
we still sometimes go in the wrong direction.
Often we know what we should do but we fail to do it.
Jesus Christ, forgive us.
Forgive us, O God, and be as kind to us
as you were to the people of old.
In the name of the Christ.

Amen.

ASSURANCE OF PARDON

The Bible is lifted high among the people.

Hear the word to us in Jesus Christ.
Our sins are forgiven.
God loves us as we are, with all our failures.
Let us live as though this is a new day.
Thanks be to God.

The Bible is returned to the holy table.

READINGS

Let us hear the word of God for us today,
that the light of Christ may shine forth on our path.

A candle is lit beside the Bible.
Readings that are appropriate to the season or context can be chosen.
Or you can choose hopeful readings such as:
Colossians 3:12-17
Ephesians 1:15-19

In this is the Word of life.
Thanks be to God.

THE REFLECTION

THE AFFIRMATION OF FAITH

In response to the word, let us affirm our faith.
In our time, and all time,
God speaks to the people in every age
through the Holy Bible,
the sacred text of the church.
This we believe.

In our time, as in every time,
God the Creator makes all things new,
breaking open buds of understanding from ancient texts,
shaking the things we thought we knew
with surprising new ideas,
that we may grow in grace.
This we believe.

A bud is placed beside the Bible.

In our time, and in every time,
Christ Jesus walks among the people,
speaking through the word in gospel books,
calling us to follow down roads of harder times
and leading us on into stronger, clearer life.
This we believe.

A cross is placed beside the Bible.

In our time, and in every time,
the Spirit lights the flame of truth
in psalm and prophet, apostle and people,
warming the world with wisdom and love,
with promises of a future beyond our sight,
and the endless company of a loving God.
This we believe.
Thanks be to God.

A bowl of charcoal is lit and placed by the Bible;
or a bright red cloth is spread around it.

PRAYERS OF INTERCESSION

Eternal God,
over the centuries your people have prayed to you in faith.
Like Abraham and Sarah, Moses and Miriam,
Mary and Peter, Paul and Phoebe,
we bring our prayers today.
As they believed that you would hear them,
we believe that you will hear us now.
We wait in hope to know your love for us
and for the world around us.
We remember, in particular, these people and situations today.

Reach out to them with streams of grace and compassion.

May your word live among them with justice, courage and truth.

*Prayers are said and, as each prayer is made, a ribbon is spread from the Bible
onto the cloth which is flowing through the centre.*

O God, we also need your comfort and encouragement.
We pray for ourselves and for each other,
bringing before you situations that are known
or that lie within our hearts in quiet need.
Reach out to us with streams of grace and compassion.
May your word live among us with wisdom, courage and truth.
Hold all life within your gracious love, O God.
May our lives show the truth of your holy word,
showing your hope,
listening for your truth,

**hearing with your compassion,
speaking with your kindness
and bravely taking our stand for all that is right.
In the name of the Christ, who is our living word.**

Amen.

THE COMMISSIONING

The Bible is lifted up and carried to the doorway.

Let us take the word of God beyond the sanctuary
and into a world which waits and longs for its coming.

BLESSING

And may the truth spring forth from each page we read,
the Christ walk beside us in each vivid story
and the Holy Spirit sing in each word we hear,
that the Holy God may be known in grace in all the earth.

Amen.

Suitable for 14–18 year-olds

DON'T JUST STAND THERE

For this service, you will need:
A large candle
A long 'pathway' cloth
Small tea candles or small candles in holders

GREETING

Christ be with you.
And also with you.

CALL TO WORSHIP

The awe of it, the wonder of it!

God's call comes to us,
as ordinary fragile people.

The awe of it, the wonder of it!

God in Christ speaks to the world,
deep in the souls of all who love him.

The awe of it, the wonder of it!
The Spirit of God is with us and within us,
leading us on into the future.

Let us worship God!

The candle is lit.

PRAYER OF INVOCATION

Dear God, in Jesus Christ,
you were so present to your first disciples
that they were afraid to have you leave them;
so close to them
that they could not imagine surviving without you.

Be as near to us as that, Jesus Christ,
be so near that we will never let you go.

Amen.

PRAYERS OF CONFESSION

God of dreams for all creation,
God of visions for a world which is yet to be,
forgive us when our dreams and visions are much smaller.
Forgive us if we just stand here looking at things,
instead of moving with the inspiration and courage of your Spirit.

Silent reflection

Forgive us, loving Jesus.

**We are sorry when we fail you.
Forgive us, loving God,
and sing a new song within us.**

Amen.

ASSURANCE OF PARDON

Jesus said that we will never be left without love,
the love of grace and forgiveness,
the love of new possibilities for us and in us.
We are forgiven!
Let us rise and take up our lives again.

Amen.

READINGS

Acts 1:6-14
John 17:1-11

REFLECTION

In the gospel passage, Jesus is obviously doing the handover to his disciples.
The future now depends on them, people who are going to be filled with
grief and loss as they face the death of Jesus. In the Acts passage, the early
church is faced with inaction in response to need and the bringing in of

justice. It has been sitting on its hands, expecting that its leaders will do everything. The leaders say, 'Over to you, folks!' and the tasks are taken up.

The truth has always been that the moment for accepting the responsibility of carrying the gospel is often not one of our choosing – it may come to us at our lowest moment rather than when we are feeling hopeful and strong. The call always comes to the whole body of Christ. It is not enough for us to talk about 'them' not doing something or that 'they' will and should be responsible. It is 'us' and 'we', or 'I' and 'me', who are always the ones who are called, in all our inadequacy, all our humanness. That is the hard truth of it and that is the wonder of it.

I am sure that you, like me, look at the problems of the world and it all seems so huge that we don't know where to start, so mostly we don't start. Someone wisely said that you only need to 'take hold of the near edge' and do your small bit. I always ask myself, 'What do I care most about? What do I feel passionate about? What is one thing that would need to change to make the world a more loving and just place?' Then I ask, 'What beginning thing can I do to connect myself with that? Who else cares about that – maybe I could join them?'

God never expects us to be Jesus Christ, to save the world, just to be our ordinary selves, doing what we can do. If we all did that, things would begin to change for the better. Often we won't even see the changes, but we are part of God's greater plan for the future.

AFFIRMATION OF FAITH

One way of affirming your faith is to make a commitment to do something or to care genuinely about something or pray for something.
As our affirmation of faith today,
let us spread this cloth from the candle which is the sign of Christ with us and down the aisle like a pathway of life.

The cloth is spread.

Now let us reflect on some small commitment we may want to make and, if we choose to do so, come and take a small candle, light it and place it on the cloth as a sign that we are tiny glimpses of the light of Christ in the world and have committed ourselves to being that.

The young people do so.

PRAYERS OF INTERCESSION

O God, who reminds us that there is no love without action,
who died to show us the greatness of your love for the world,
raise up in us a new energy for bringing in the changes
so that your love may be believed,
and so that our love for the world may be believed.
Encourage us so that we are able to stay hopeful
when nothing seems to happen.
Give to us a sense of your grand dream
and our place in that among the people
who try to work for good over the centuries.

Travel with us on our journey, brave Jesus.
Never leave us alone.

And now let us remember people who need our prayers.
Let us say the names of the people or the situations about which we care
most.

The people do so.

Gather up all that we bring with all that you bring to our life, O God.

Inspire us to go on in our efforts to be your true people,
that many may know that you have come into the world.

Amen.

SENDING OUT AND BLESSING

Look at the world with eyes of love and hear its cries with ears of concern.
Then, go into the world as those who don't just stand there, but do
something,
for we are the children of God.
And may God be with us forever,
Christ be our friend,
and the Spirit guide our feet.

Amen.

HARD QUESTIONS

For this service, you will need:
Small pieces of paper and pencils for each person to be given at the door
A bare branch of a tree in a pot
A large flat bowl with a sprinkling of earth in it
A basket of leaves

GREETING

Christ be with you.
And also with you.

OPENING

In the hard times of life,
in the centre of our unanswered questions
when everything feels as cold as winter,
with flowers and leaves fallen by the wayside,
there is God among the fallen blossomings,
like steel in the centre of the still-standing tree,
flowing forth in the waters of our anxious thoughts
and gently, tenderly, holding us all in love.

The tree branch is carried to the table.

IN FAITH WE COME

In faith, O God,
we dare to bring to you the doubts, the questions,
the anxieties, the angers and the pain
which are part of our journey through life.
We place them all in honesty into your hands
for your care and compassion.

Silent reflection

We are sorry if we have kept them from you,
as though we are afraid of your anger,
or because we can find no answers.

Silent reflection

In faith we come, as we are,
as we have been and as we may be,
for you are our God
and we are your people.
In the name of Jesus Christ.

Amen.

READING

Revelation 22:1-5

REFLECTION

God is never afraid of our questions or angry that we are asking them.
The people of God, as we can read in the Bible, have always cried out to God
when things are hard or puzzling or full of pain and grief.

· Give some honest examples of your own hard questions for God and some
  possible questions which may be in the hearts of the young people.

When we listen to Bible passages like the one in Revelation, it is to remind us
that, in the end, God is working towards a better day for all people and caring
for us as we go, just like a special healing tree which stands each side of our
life all the way. This tree does not save us from all sorts of problems or painful
times. It reminds us that God weeps with us and is angry with those who hurt
us. It is there, caring for us, reaching out towards us with healing leaves.

God travels with us through every single thing that happens to us and never
leaves us alone. That may not seem enough, but it is. The company of God
lifts us up in hope, comforts us in sorrow and gives us strength and courage
to go on.

OUR QUESTIONS

On the pieces of paper that you received as you came in, I invite you to write down your hard questions for God and during the prayer to place them in the bowl of earth and cover them gently with the leaves from the basket.

WE PRAY

As the night kindly covers the earth with its restfulness,
and the tree of life waits quietly and hopefully for the day,
so we rest in your love, O God.

Silent prayer

We have gathered up the hard questions in our lives:

the things we don't understand,
the things we think are unfair,
questions about why life is as it is,
things that make us angry or hurt
and we will place them under the leaves of the tree
for your healing, wisdom and grace.

The young people place their prayers and questions.

These are our honest and earthy questions, O God.
We leave them under the leaves and hope for your healing.
We leave them there and pray for greater understanding.
We leave them and ask for your comfort in all that we face.

**We will watch for the buds of new possibilities
and help each other when life is tough
until we know more or can believe more.**

Silent reflection

We know that you will never leave us alone, loving God.

**Help us in our times of unbelief,
lead us to your living water
and call us to the kindness of peace under the tree of life.**

Amen.

SENDING OUT AND BLESSING

Go out in faith and dare to keep asking
your honest questions of a loving God.

And may the winters of life
be filled with the warm light of the Spirit,
the promise of God be around you
like the emerging of spring,
and Jesus be discovered waiting for you
at every bend in the road.

Amen.

Suitable for 12–18 year-olds

LIVING WATER

For this service, you will need:
A flowing blue cloth with which to dress the table
A large jug of water on the table
A large bowl, either on the table or the floor, into which to pour the water
Small cups – individual communion glasses would be suitable or disposable cups
used for medication

GREETING

Christ be with you.
And also with you.

CALL TO WORSHIP

God, who stands under us like a rock,
calm and still in the midst of our trembling life,

we worship you.

Jesus Christ, who holds out hands of care
in the midst of our wanderings,

we worship you.

God, from whose being springs the water of poured-out life,
flowing over the world in endless blessing,

we worship you and we open our hearts to your gifts this day.

PRAYER OF CONFESSION

Loving Jesus, you offer us your gifts so that we may live fully.
If we choose to live with caution,
to live a little, rather than to live much,
to keep things as they are,

forgive us and open our eyes to the truth.
Forgive us and bring us into your abundant life.

Amen.

ASSURANCE OF FORGIVENESS

The water of life is the water of grace.
Even when we are truly known in all our weakness and failure,
we are loved of God.
We are forgiven!

Thanks be to God.

READINGS

Exodus 17:1-6

In this is the word for us.
Thanks be to God.

John 4:5-30

This is the gospel of Christ.
Praise to you, Lord Jesus Christ.

REFLECTION

As we pour this water into the bowl,
let us image the offering of the woman at the well to Jesus
and his offering of living water to her.

The water is poured.

This story has many messages in it. We can see that Jesus is a person who looks for gifts from all sorts of unlikely people – those whom other people pass by as having little to offer.

Or we can think about what 'living water' means. I think it is about the gifts that God gives to us in many different ways – gifts that help us to live more strongly. Living water – the strength we receive if we will reach out and invite God to be with us, gives us new moments of courage and wisdom and energy for good.

I can think of many occasions in my life when things were tough and I have said to God, 'I have nothing left to offer' and I have felt something being given to me. Sometimes, it has felt just like being given a drink of cool water. Sometimes, it has been in the form of a friend reaching out towards me and giving support. Other times, it has been like a new thought in my head which clarifies things for me or simply a sense that I need not go on struggling without stopping. I can take a break, rest and be restored.

I am sure you can think of such times. Often we need reminding to stop, to wait, to ask and to expect that God can be with us and give us this living water.

PRAYERS FOR OTHERS AND OURSELVES

O God, we have tasted the tears of the world in many places,
the water of the weeping of suffering places and people.
We pray for all those whose need is great.
As they thirst for peace,

bring them our commitment to end all violence.

As they thirst for food,

fill them from the overflowing plates of the world.

As they thirst for justice,

lift up our courage to end oppression.

As they thirst for love,

give us arms to embrace the lonely.

We too thirst, O God.
Let us reflect on what we have to offer
and what we need from Jesus.
If you would like to do so,
come and take a cup of water from the bowl,
return to your seat and, as you drink it,
pray for your own life and the living water you need.

The young people do so.

O God, we always thirst for more wisdom in being your people,
more courage in being there for others,

more faith in being those
who are called to change the world into a better place,
more love in being the ones who show others your love,
and more gentleness with each other
as we try to do what we know we should do
in becoming the children of God.
Give to us your living water every day,
that we may never thirst again.

Amen.

SENDING OUT AND BLESSING

Go into the world as those who drink
at the fountain of truth and life.
And may God be found standing on a rock
in all the hard places,
breaking open the streams of life before us
and leading us on in faith.

Amen.

Suitable for 12–18 year-olds

MYSTERY ON A MOUNTAIN

For this service, you will need:
A shining cloth – gold lamé is best
Strips of bright ribbon in a basket

CALL TO WORSHIP

God who comes to us in the mountains of our life,
in the times when we stop and look
for shining hopes and awesome possibilities,

at this time of new beginnings,
we come in faith
to discover new ways forward in our lives.

The shining cloth is spread from the table down the centre aisle.

CONFESSION

Holy God, sometimes we would rather not know
your hopes for us;
we would rather stay as we are
without the challenge of changes.

Silent reflection

Other times we choose not to listen to you

and simply to please ourselves
and go in our own directions.

Silent reflection

Forgive us, O God,
and call us back to your presence.

Amen.

ASSURANCE OF FORGIVENESS

Jesus Christ never leaves us alone.
Here, in this place,
there is a mountaintop gift of grace for us.
In Christ we are forgiven.
Rise up and live!

Amen.

READINGS

Psalm 99
Matthew 17:1-9

REFLECTION

- Sometimes the mystery on the mountain that is God's gift to us is a moment of awe and wonder that carries us beyond ourselves into an experience of healing and energy, new peace or new insight about something.

- That gives us an idea of the sort of place that is a good place to go or to remember when we need new energy and new hope.

- When the disciples saw Jesus, their friend whom they thought they knew, looking like God in front of them, they hardly knew what to do.

  They thought maybe they should stay there on the mountaintop and worship Jesus.

- However, he took them down the mountain and showed them that the real Christian life is lived mostly at the bottom of things, among all sorts of people who need the love and healing of God.

- Here is an experience of being 'brought down the mountain' and faced with life at the bottom. A woman was chairing the Worship Committee for the Harare Assembly of the World Council of Churches and was very focused on the worship of God. She was staying in a student residence at the University of Harare. For the Assembly, this was to be cleaned by the normally unemployed women of the Widows' Association of Harare. Night and day they cleaned the corridors, the rooms and the bathrooms, working long hours for very little pay. They were welcoming women, kindly to the delegates as visitors to their city. Each day, most people went off to their meals and the WCC meetings and left them to do the cleaning. One morning the woman returned to get something from her room in the middle of the morning. As she approached the bathroom nearby, she heard unusual noises – ecstatic noises, sounds of happiness, with much laughter and some singing. She looked in the door and there were the cleaning women, clutching tiny fragments of soap, bathing and showering in joy and delight. They were lifting up their arms to feel the water flowing over their bodies, almost dancing under the showers and lying back in the full bath in bliss, encouraging each other in this wondrous moment of access to running water, hot running water! When they saw her, the sounds suddenly stopped and then they all laughed together, celebrating the moment and her recognition that they had 'seized their day' against the odds. They reminded her that there, among the glorious worship which was being held nearby, were women who never knew the joy and justice of access to running water.

- This story about Jesus also reminds us that sometimes we see people every day but never really see them deeply. Then one day, we receive the gift of seeing that person in a beautiful way – one in which we have never seen them before.

- It also reminds us that sometimes it is good to go to the place where we feel a sense of awe and wonder and feel again a special presence of God.

MYSTERY ON THE MOUNTAIN

Quiet, reflective music is played.

As we hear this music, let us see if we can remember
a place or a moment when we received this gift,
as did the disciples on the mountain.
It may not be an image of Jesus that we see,
just a sense of being connected with some energy or presence
which lies beyond ourselves and is greater than us.
It may simply be a sense of awe and being somewhere special and uplifting.

You may like to honour that experience by taking a bright stream of ribbon from the basket and placing it on the cloth as a sign that you too have transforming moments, gifts from God.

The young people do so.

PRAYERS OF INTERCESSION

We thank you, God,
that you are not a boring dreary God,
but one who is full of surprises,
the one who transforms people and situations.

Shine your light on the world
and show us what is true and good.
Shine your light and hope
when people despair of ever living in a kinder world,
where people lose sight of anything that is good,
where people look at each other and see little of worth.

Place the light of your life around us all.

so that we may see each other as special people
standing in the light of your love for us.

A silence is kept.

Come to us this day, O Jesus.

Come to us, for we long to meet you.

Amen.

COMMISSIONING

Walk free into the clouds which cover the mountains of life,
and discover our God waiting in a mystery of grace and love.

BLESSING

And may Jesus Christ stand before you in joy,
God the loving parent of us all speak from the skies over you,
and the Spirit hold your hand as you enter the life
that lies spread out below.

Amen.

Suitable for 14 –18 year-olds

TEMPTATIONS

For this service, you will need:

A pen or pencil for each person
A sheet of paper attached to each order of service (Stick-on notes are good)
A basket to receive the sheets of paper

GREETING

Christ be with you.
And also with you.

CALL TO WORSHIP

God in Jesus who gives us choices,
honours us as friends rather than servants
and calls us into tough decisions,

we worship you.

God in Jesus who lives out the challenge of life with us,
who is not sitting in some distant heaven
and watching our struggles,

we worship you.

God for every moment, every day, every year,

we worship you.

CONFESSION

Dear Jesus, you were tempted as we are tempted,
and you feel for us with a human heart,
because you have walked this earth like us,
we come to share our lives with you today.
Sometimes, we would rather have less freedom

when the choices are hard.
We would rather you told us what to do
so that we do not have to make the decision ourselves.

Silent reflection

Then sometimes, dear Jesus, we are tempted,
just as you were tempted,
to do grand and powerful things so that people will think we are special.

**Forgive us and restore us, O God,
heal us and call us into life.**

Amen.

ASSURANCE OF FORGIVENESS

This is our God, the one who understands
and forgives our failures and fears.
We are forgiven!

We are called to live fully and freely as the friends of God.

Amen.

READINGS

Genesis 2:15-17; 3:1-7

In this is the word of the Lord.
Thanks be to God.

Matthew 4:1-11

This is the gospel of Jesus Christ.
Praise to you, Lord Jesus Christ.

REFLECTION

As with all other passages of Scripture, there are layers of meaning and
message for us.

We are all very familiar with the story of Adam and Eve and its mystery. If
you read it all carefully, it really looks as though it was about an early tribe
trying to understand why people had to endure suffering – in childbirth

– and endless hard work for survival. It was also about a moment of deep awareness when people realised that they could act as God and do what they liked.
But let us concentrate more on the temptations of Jesus.
• Jesus is led into the wilderness.
A place where there are few resources and where he has no option but to connect with himself, a place where, at a low point in energy and company, he is tempted.
• The nature of his temptations is interesting.
He is tempted to do magic things to show his power – making stones into bread and dramatically throwing himself off a great height for angels to catch.
Both these activities would have won him great applause and a large following.
And he would have done a great deal of good.

Have you ever wondered why God doesn't simply arrange for the hungry to be fed and to convert everyone to the worship of God by doing lots of marvellous things?
Surely if God is almighty, this is possible?
I think it is, but the truth is that if our love could be bought by the good deeds of God, the relationship with God would be seriously distorted.
• Then he is tempted to sell his soul in order to rule the world.
You can imagine that it is possible to persuade God that he would rule in justice and love, but Jesus was not prepared to pay the price of getting to that.

I believe that there are understandings of the limits that God places on Godself in this story so that the dignity of human freedom and responsibility will not be destroyed and so that we will have a relationship with God that is uncluttered by rewards.

There are also messages for us that have to do with the perils of temptations to be corrupted by power, even if you start out on the right track with concern for others and for the prevailing of good. This is really the peril of perhaps the greatest sin of all – that of beginning to think you are God or more righteous or special than other people.

Many of us have our own stories of temptations around playing with power… I know that I do and that it was only the love of brave friends who dared to tell me that I was becoming too fond of power – 'up myself' as you might say – that made me stop and think very hard. It was a long journey to the place where Jesus arrived – the place where I saw that power over people and being 'important' made me less of a person rather than a larger person. I found it very comforting that Jesus went through the same temptation.

PRAYERS FOR OTHERS AND OURSELVES

Let us spend a time of quiet while we think about
the hardest temptations that we face ourselves.
On the pieces of paper that were attached to your order of service,
you may like to write your own prayer,
asking God to give you strength in relation to particular temptations.
Then you are invited to come and place your prayer in this basket
that stands before the cross,
or simply take it with you when you go.

The young people do so.

Let us all pray.

Loving God,
help us to know more clearly
which are the pathways towards good.

Silent prayer

Send your holy presence of truth
to stand beside us and all who struggle
to carry forward the work of justice and peace in a struggling world.
Stand with the flame of your costly love beside those who suffer.

Silent prayer

Together we pray:

In our times of freedom, be present with us, Holy Spirit of God.
In our times of responsibility, be clearly by our side, Jesus Christ.
In our times of aloneness in the face of life and its decisions,
hold us in your loving arms, O God,
for we pray in your name.

Amen.

SENDING OUT AND BLESSING

Go forth in faith, even into the wilderness.
Go in peace, because Jesus Christ is with us.
And may the Spirit lift your life into flights of glorious freedom,
the breath of God carry you towards the new heaven and new earth,
and the Christ place your feet on the ground in earthy truth.

Amen.

Suitable for 12–18 year-olds

THE COMING OF THE SPIRIT

For this service, you will need:

A flame-shaped red candle or a series of different red candles arranged in a group
A long red cloth
All sorts of symbols of beauty and hope, eg flowers, beautiful stones or coloured ribbons, beautiful leaves, photos of people we love, pictures of good situations or paintings that celebrate life, small plants growing (see prayer of thanksgiving)
A small bird (can often be found in craft shops)

GREETING
Christ be with you.
And also with you.

CALL TO WORSHIP
Our past is gathered up in love,

for the Spirit of God was always with us.

Our present is lived in the company of God,

for the Spirit of God is always with us.

Our future will never be faced alone,

for the Spirit of God will always be with us.
Praise be to God! The Holy Spirit has come!

The flame candle is lit or the series of red candles.

INVITING GOD TO BE WITH US
As we remember the day of Pentecost,
speak to us in our own language, Holy Spirit.
Be like a bright tongue of flame on our heads this day, we pray,

and blow through our lives as a wind of freedom and truth, O God.

Show us again that we are with you and you are with us.

Amen.

PRAYER OF CONFESSION

Dear God, who touches our spirit with your Spirit,
we confess that there are times
when we do not know what we do not know.
We go stumbling on in our life,
with our own fixed ideas,
taking little notice of ideas that come from others
and that could be your voice to us.
Sometimes we even close off the longings in our own hearts
as though you could only love parts of us.

Silence

Sometimes we confess that our lives
show little of the joy of your delighted life.
Forgive us, O God,

and restore your Spirit in passionate life within us.

Amen.

ASSURANCE OF PARDON

The waiting is over.
The Spirit of God, the healer, forgiver and lover of our lives,
is set free in all the earth, spreading the truth of the grace of God.
Open your lives to receive the Spirit.

Forgiveness is ours!
Thanks be to God!

READINGS

Acts 2:1-21
John 14:8-17

REFLECTION

The coming of the Spirit is like a reaching out of the life of God towards us.
This life of God is always moving towards us, seeking to come through into our life
  • beyond any feelings of guilt we have, or our grieving, powerlessness, hopelessness, humiliations, betrayals, doubts or confusions.
On the day of Pentecost, no-one was missed out.
  • Each one was surprised by God.
  • No-one was beyond the reach of the loving Spirit of God.
  • It was intoxicating! It was marvellous!
It was deeply real – far beyond a sort of intellectual knowing or a believing in some set of rules or beliefs for faith.
It reached into the hearts and souls of all present:
  • meeting them where they were, not where they ought to be,
  • speaking in ways which were in their own language, their own ways of thinking and understanding.
To let that happen to us is to be open to life and love which is beyond human understanding.

PRAYER OF THANKSGIVING

A long red cloth is swirled around the candle/s and down the aisle towards the people, and symbols of beauty and hope are placed upon it.

Thank you, bright Spirit, for the melodies in your song to us,
your calling into lightness of heart and soul in a troubled world.
Thank you, bright Spirit, for all the signs of God around us
in colour and flowerings, in sunlight on water and calm of the sea,
in boldness of mountain peaks and shadows on stone,
in poetry and painting, in music and in dancing,
in courage and caring, in hope and faith,
as we live in the creativity and joy of your image, O God.
Amen.

PRAYERS OF INTERCESSION

A small bird is held out towards the people.

Come down, dove of peace, Spirit of God.
Be imaged in the birds of the air as they fly near to our life

and make every birdsong sound to us like the notes of your hope.
Call the whole world into the soaring wonder of your freeing life
as you enter with us the adventure of faith.

Silent prayer

Stand under our life, Spirit of God.
Speak to us from the ground beneath our feet,
and come forth from the mystery of the deep places of the earth.
Warm and shake our life with the fire of your Spirit which never goes out
in its passion for the healing and renewing of all things.

Silent prayer

Speak to us, Spirit of God, wisdom of the ages,
stirring within us as new truth,
sounding in the voices of the good in each generation.

Silent prayer

Come, Spirit of love, and warm our hearts with loving kindness
for all the world and for the creation itself.
As our hearts are warmed,
we pray for those whom we know need love at this moment:

The people pray, passing the bird to each other as they bring their prayers.

Come, Holy Spirit, companion in our shadows
and dancer in the light.

Come, Holy Spirit, to all your creation.

Amen.

SENDING OUT AND BLESSING

Carry the Spirit of God into the world.
Lift high the bringer of truth!
Go with open hands because the Spirit is received,
but never held in our grasp.

And may the rays of every sunrise remind us of the sign of the Spirit's flame,
the restful dark of night be the Spirit's gift of peace to us
and that which lies between be safely held in the hands of God.
Amen.

Suitable for 12–18 year-olds

THE WORLD – A SACRED SPACE

For this service, you will need:
A large candle on the table
A flat earthen bowl and a smaller bowl of earth alongside it
Seeds

GREETING

Christ be with you.
And also with you.

Welcome to this sacred space,
a space where we might come close to our God,
close to our world and close to each other.

Silence

CALL TO WORSHIP

The flame of the life of God is lit again and again
in the sacred ground of this our world.

The candle is lit.

The life of Christ has walked our earthly way
and declared our humanness as a sacred place.

A large earthen bowl is placed before the candle.

The Spirit sows seeds of love among us
and they will form a tree of life for all.

Let us worship our God!

PRAYER OF CONFESSION

Let us enter a time of confession, of grieving, before our God.
O God, there are many times when we fail to see,
or hear, or touch, or understand things around us
which are important and part of your special creation.
There, on this the sacred ground of your world,
was a trembling living thing – and we did not see it.

Silent reflection

There, was a cry of longing and loneliness – and we did not hear it.

Silent reflection

There, when we needed someone,
was a hand stretched out towards us – and we did not touch it.

Silent reflection

Gracious God, forgive us.

**Forgive us,
for we stand in sadness on this, your sacred ground.**

ASSURANCE OF PARDON

God in Jesus Christ is always standing with us on the ground,
giving us love and forgiveness,
calling us on to live kindly with the whole creation.

Thanks be to God!

READINGS

Isaiah 42:5-9
Mark 4:26-30

REFLECTION

· It is encouraging to think that the reign of God can begin with small things
  – tiny seeds of life which we don't even recognise as the beginning of
  something much larger and more significant.

· It is hard for us to imagine that our little lives could be part of something in
  God's plan for the world.

- The encouraging thing is that we may only be the beginning of something which others water like a seed and care for and make grow into something fruitful and beautiful.
- Sometimes we can watch for a seed already growing and be the one who does the encouraging.
- The little things are never wasted in God's dream for the world and that good things can begin with us, right where we live.
- Our life and our place is sacred ground.

AFFIRMATION AND INTERCESSION

Let us say what we believe and bring our prayers for others
to our loving God:
We believe that every place
is the sacred ground of your creation, O God.
You are always there before us; you are always there beside us,
and you will walk the way ahead of us.

**Bless, we pray, the sacred ground of the world
where we live and work.**

We place this earth in the bowl
and we name our own sacred ground before our God.
Let us name the places where we live.

*The people name the places where they live
as earth is sprinkled into the bowl.*

We remember other places around the world
which is also your sacred ground
and we pray that the seeds of your justice and love will be discovered there.

The people name the places and seeds are sprinkled on the earth.

Open our eyes so that we may see your tree of life,
growing from small things into spreading branches of good and gentleness.
Make us part of your love so that people can shelter beside us,
for healing and care.

We pray this in the name of Jesus.

Amen.

BLESSING

Go into this day in faith
to discover the presence of God in each person and place.
And may the hand of God hold you tenderly,
the Christ walk beside you,
and the Spirit light the path ahead.

Amen.

GRIEVING A SUICIDE

Tragically, people who suicide are often young people. This leaves their friends at school or in a youth group devastated, sometimes full of guilt, sometimes even attracted to death as a form of dealing with life. Sometimes they have not been able to go to the funeral or the funeral has not dealt with the fact that the person died through suicide. This is a service which can be used to help them work with the consequences of a friend who suicided.

For this service, you will need:
A large bowl of water to be placed on a central table or on a cloth flowing from a table
Loose flowers in a basket

OPENING

We have come together
because we loved *Name*.
Here we will mourn him/her leaving us,
honour his/her life,
and comfort each other.
We come, believing that all human life is valuable,
that the truth and integrity and hopefulness
which lies in each life, lives on.
We come, believing that *Name's* life,
which we remember today
and for which we now experience great loss,
is joined with all life,
stretching into the past and into the future.
His/her life was lived in its uniqueness with us
and now rests secure in the loving hands of God.

PRAYER

O God, at this moment, as we come face to face with death,
especially this tragic death,

we have many feelings alongside our grief.
Please come close to us with your love,
travel with us into this harsh moment
and open our hearts to each other.
We ask it in the name of Jesus Christ,
who faced his own death and the death of a friend.

Amen.

Name chose the manner and the time of his/her dying
and this is hard for us to face.
In our grief, we ask ourselves whether,
if had we been different people,
or done something more for him/her,
he/she would have stayed longer with us
and chosen a gentler death.
There will never be enough tears to express our pain
as we recognise his/her pain at the ending of his/her life.
But the truth is that, in our humanness, there are times
when we will never have enough to offer some people,
never enough to give to them to hold them into life.

We place this bowl of water, the sign of our weeping,
at the centre of our life today.

The bowl is placed on the table.

READING

Revelation 21:1-6

REFLECTION

We may live with the questions forever, but the word for us at this moment
is that all that is ever required of us is that we do our best in loving each
other and in responding to each other's needs. This we have done in all
integrity, both as family, friends and as a community of faith.

We are therefore called to receive forgiveness if we feel that is needed
and open our lives to the healing and comfort of God.
We are called to live our lives in peace and trust in the grace of God
and the generosity of *Name* himself/herself,

a gift which we have all received in many forms over the years.

Let us now begin, in faith and hope,
to lay down the difficult things which lie in the past
and be open to the gift of the love and understanding of God.

A silence is kept.

The gifts and graces that *Name* offered
must never be lost to us in the pain of his/her dying.
The creativity that he/she brought to us
in his/her life and relationships lies now within our own lives
and travels into the future with us.
Our lives are more beautiful because we lived with *Name*.

None of us knows the whole truth about what lies beyond death. Christians believe that as we journey between life and death, we are safe in the hands of an infinitely gracious God.

The God who stands with us at that moment is the same God who was prepared to die in love for all humankind, a God who has entered every struggle of our life with us and who deeply understands the choices we have made.

REMEMBERING NAME'S LIFE

As each person speaks about Name, *they place a flower into the bowl of water with the words:*

In Jesus Christ, the water of our tears will become living water for the ongoing of life.

Let us pray or reflect in silence on this life and what it has meant to us.

Silent prayer/reflection

Thanks be to God for the gifts we have received in *Name*.
Perhaps *Name* is here with us now in spirit.
I will say out loud some of the thoughts that lie in our hearts.
Name, we will always wish you had stayed much longer with us
and that you had not chosen to die in this way,
but we will now set you free as you travel on into a new day.
We will always remember you and all that you have given to us in your short life and we will value who you were for us.

To love someone is to risk the pain of parting.
Not to love is never to have lived.
The grief which we now experience is the honouring of our love.
Let us now in a quiet moment make our farewell to *Name*.

Silence

PRAYER

O God, we pray that you will care for *Name*
in ways which we have not been able to do,
and that your love will be with us now
and with all who grieve the loss of family or friend.
Give us your gifts so that we are able to take up our lives
in ways which are strong and true
and which carry us into the hope of the future.
We pray in the name of Jesus Christ, who wept for the loss of a friend.

Amen.

SENDING OUT AND BLESSING

And now let us go into the world,
glad that we have loved,
free to weep for the one we have lost,
free to hold each other in our human frailty,
empowered to live life to the full
and to affirm the hope of human existence.
And may God be our company,
Christ Jesus walk before us,
and the Spirit surround us with a cloud of grace.

Amen.

Suitable for 12–18 year olds

COMING TO LIFE

For this service, you will need:
A large glass bowl of water, representing our tears
A light cloth to cover the bowl
A free-standing cross
A basket of cut flowers

GREETING

Christ be with you.
And also with you.

CALL TO WORSHIP

When we feel lost and dead inside,

our hope is in God.

When people we love die or leave us,

our hope is in God.

When the world around us seems full of despair,

our hope is in God,
the God who makes all things possible.
Let us worship God.

THE WEEPING

Sometimes our lives have hidden tears.
A bowl of tears is placed on the table.
They are covered over with things like our pride,
our sense that no-one would care for us
or that we should be stronger or better than we are.

The bowl is covered.

PRAYER OF CONFESSION

Come, Holy Spirit, come.
Come, gentle Jesus, come to us.
Come, great Creator, be with us
as we stand and look at the things which we fear,
the things we worry about.

Silent reflection

Forgive us, loving Jesus.

**Forgive us if we find it hard to believe
that you weep with us when life is hard.**

Amen.

ASSURANCE OF FORGIVENESS

Jesus said, 'I am come
that you may have life and have it to the full'.
This is the promise to us and the centre of our faith.
Receive the forgiveness of God.
Live as though your God loves you as you are.

Thanks be to God.

The bowl is uncovered.

READING

John 11:1-6, 17-45
This is the gospel of Jesus Christ.

Praise to you, Lord Jesus Christ.

REFLECTION

We don't really know much about this story.
Jesus may literally have raised his friend Lazarus from the dead.
On the other hand, if he did, why were the disciples so amazed when Jesus
rose from the dead? We never hear of Lazarus again, which is surprising
seeing he had been dead and was then alive again – you would think he
would be famous!

In the time when the Bible was written, people often wrote things differently to the way we do today. They wrote to tell something very important in dramatic ways, rather than telling us exactly what happened.

Possibly the real meaning of this story is that Jesus loved people just as much as we do. He had close friends and he wept when they died. He probably wished he had come earlier to say goodbye to Lazarus instead of staying the extra days where he was.

What Jesus said to the family of Lazarus when he came out of the tomb was, 'Unbind him and let him go'. Maybe he was telling them to free Lazarus to continue his journey after death – to let him go with their love and the love of Jesus going with him. Sometimes we need to do that, with great sadness, but confident that the person is safe in the loving hands of God.

Sometimes we have to let all sorts of things go, in order to be free ourselves – things like

- people we wish were still our friends
- ideas about ourselves which are no longer true
- guilt about things we have done
- guilt about things we did not do but wish we had done

It is hard to let things go in order to live with freedom, and sometimes it takes time and we just need to cry about it for a while before we can move on. Jesus is always there for us, understanding our journey and our struggles.

PRAYERS OF INTERCESSION

Jesus Christ never leaves us alone.
The cross of Christ reminds us that Jesus
has entered our human journey and our weeping.
A cross is placed near the bowl of tears.
Jesus Christ, hope of the world,
weep with the world this day, we pray.
There are so many people and situations
where people are struggling or in pain.
We especially remember those who have lost loved ones –
a mother or a father, a sister or a brother –
and who are finding it hard to go on, so great is their loss.

Silent refection

Let us call out particular people or situations
which we want to remember
and place a flower in the bowl of tears as a sign of our love.

The people do so.

Loving Jesus, we also pray for ourselves,
for all the people here and for those who love us.
You know best if any of us are sad
or feeling that life is hard for us.

Be our friend, Jesus Christ, and weep with us.
Comfort those who need comfort
and bring new life among us.

Amen.

SENDING OUT AND BLESSING

Go into the world as those who are alive and free
and filled with the wonder of the power of God for good.

And may the whole earth be filled with songs of hope,
trusting in its true source of life,
and trembling in awe as it recognises
its Comforter, its Maker, and its Friend.

Amen.

FAMILY SERVICES

Family Service

LOVE IS OUR THEME

For this service, you will need:

A candle

Long strips of paper people – the sort you make by folding a strip of paper and cutting out a stick figure then unfolding the paper so you have little stick figures holding hands. The young people/children can make these and stick them together so that there are enough strips for each row of seats. They can be in different colours.

Rolls of ribbon – enough to encircle the whole congregation

CALL TO WORSHIP

God is love and love is of God.

We celebrate this love.

God's love lives within us
and we open our hearts to others.

We celebrate this love.

Here in this place, among each other,
we find love in many forms.

We celebrate this love.
Let us worship God!

LIGHTING THE CANDLE

This candle is the symbol of the love of God,
a flame of light which shows us who we are
and then tenderly surrounds us with warmth
like the arms of a loving parent.

It is a light which shows us the way
towards love which never ends.

The candle is lit.

THE GRIEVING, THE CONFESSION

Gracious God, we grieve for the times when we are less than loving,
the times when we become so focused on ourselves
that we fail to notice that someone else needs our care or compassion;
the times when we simply run out of energy to care for others
and have little left to share.

Silent reflection

Forgive us, O God.

Forgive us and gift us the gift of love.

We grieve for our lack of trust in your love for us,
the times when we stay in aloneness and guilt
instead of reaching out for the grace
that you are always offering to us.

Silent reflection

Forgive us, O God.

**Forgive us and gift us the gift of love,
for we pray in the name of Jesus Christ.**

Amen.

ASSURANCE OF FORGIVENESS

Nothing in heaven or on earth
can separate us from the love of God in Christ Jesus.
We are forgiven!

Thanks be to God!

READINGS

Hosea 11:1-4, 8-9

In this is the word of the Lord.
Thanks be to God.

Luke 17:11-19

This is the gospel of Jesus Christ.
Praise to you, Lord Jesus Christ.

REFLECTION

Many of us here would see ourselves as loving people – we love each other, we love our families and we love our friends.

Jesus once said, 'So how is that so special – to love those who love you?'

Then he went on to outline that the great love to which God calls us is much wider than that – it even includes those we find it hard to love.

Often when he told stories, such as the well known 'Good Samaritan', he invited people to break through the boundaries of their loving.

When the girls who helped to create this service chose the passage about the healing of the lepers, I reflected with great thankfulness on the maturity of their understanding of loving. First, we have the picture of the lepers, regarded as unclean because of the terrible and infectious disease which they had – a band of people who lived outside normal community life. Possibly, if we put this situation in the time when it happened, we can understand to some extent why the lepers were pushed away to the outskirts of society.

In this day and age, we would put them into hospital and treat them with the medical knowledge which we have today. It is interesting to reflect on who we would send away from us today as not worthy of being part of the community.

· People who are mentally ill often live on the edges of society and are often treated with caution, even when they become well. When I worked in the centre of Sydney, a large percentage of the homeless people were mentally ill.

· People with disabilities are also often hard for us to love and relate to, especially if they look different and act strangely.

But Jesus was not prepared to leave the lepers by the roadside – he reached out and healed them. Only one leper came back to thank him, and at first it appears that the main thing that Jesus is doing is to say, 'Well, you might have said thank you!'

However, if you read carefully, you can see that his focus is really on drawing attention to the fact that, of the ten lepers, it is the Samaritan who comes back to say thanks.

The Samaritans were regarded by the Jews of that day as foreigners who were vastly inferior – no good was expected from them. Jesus is saying to his disciples, 'Look who came back and was thankful!' Love is often about seeing people differently and believing that they would have something to offer into our life together.

It is also about moving away from stereotyping people:
all Samaritans are bad
all people of other faiths are less worthy
all refugees may be terrorists
all people of other cultures have much to learn from us.

In this church, we try hard to enact the inclusive, the embracing love of God, the love like that we heard about in the book of Hosea, the God who cannot help loving and understanding people.

We do it by encouraging deep respect for families of other faiths, and celebrating cultural differences and working on imaging openness to a wider love for all people, especially those in need.

At the very centre of our faith lies the great commandment that we love one another as Christ has loved us. Overarching all of this is our faith in the love of God who gives us such grace that in thanksgiving and understanding and compassion we offer it to others.

We also believe that the way we love and contribute to human community is not simply about what we do for others but about whom we become ourselves.

OFFERING

OFFERING PRAYER

Receive our gifts, O God.
Take them and expand them,
that love may be shared between us
and with those who long for a greater love.
Amen.

PRAYERS FOR OTHERS AND OURSELVES

Dear God, we pray for all those who do not have enough love,
people who are separated from those who love them,
or who have never really had loving people around them.
We also pray for those who feel they are not loved
because they do not receive a fair share
of the world's food, clothing, work, shelter or freedom,
or because they are suffering in war.
We especially think of these people.

Prayers are shared.

Then, O God, we pray for ourselves.
We pray that we will be a centre of care
for each other and for the world beyond us.
Give to us a special understanding for those who are different among us,
or those who find it hard to ask for what they need in care or support.

**Bless our church and all its families
that it may be a living example of your loving community.
This we pray in faith.**

Amen.

LORD'S PRAYER

**Our Father in heaven,
hallowed be your name,
your kingdom come,
your will be done,
on earth as in heaven.
Give us today our daily bread.
Forgive us our sins
as we forgive those who sin against us.
Save us from the time of trial
and deliver us from evil.
For the kingdom, the power and the glory are yours
now and for ever.   Amen.**

THE SENDING OUT

The church is like a family of love.
To remind us of this, let us each take hold of
the streams of paper people,
which we will now pass along each row,
as a symbol of our life together.

The paper people are passed along the rows.

We are not only joined together in loving community,
we are also encircled by the love of God.
We will take the ribbon of encircling love
around the candle which is the sign of the love of God,
around ourselves and out into the world.

The ribbon is passed around the candle and the people.

The love of God encircles us and flows out into the world outside this place.
Let us now take one of these paper people
to remind us of our place in loving community.

The people tear off a paper person.

Now let us take this ribbon and flow it down the aisles
and out to the doors
as a sign of the love we will carry into the world.

Young people carry out the ribbon.

THE COMMITMENT

Let us make our commitment to live in loving community.
**We will go from here in faith,
to build a community of love together,
to spread that hope into all the world
and to point to the love of God for all people.**

BLESSING

May the love of God the Creator surround you,
the company of Jesus the Christ be beside you,
and the Spirit mark a pathway of grace before you.

Amen.

Family Service

MAKING CHOICES

For this service, you will need:
A flowing cloth from the communion table down the central aisle like a pathway
A candle placed on the table and means of lighting it
A cross on the table
Two large rocks
A Bible
Paper footprints

GREETING

Christ be with you.
And also with you.

CALL TO WORSHIP

God, who gives us awesome freedom to choose,

we worship you.

God, who respects our human journey,

we worship you.

God, whose Spirit never leaves us or forsakes us,

as we make our choices,
we worship you this day.

MAKING CHOICES

When we make difficult choices, we travel a pathway towards our decision.
Each great religion has its own pathway
in the search for each moment of truth in life.
We walk respectfully alongside each other in doing that.
In this service, we will image our travelling along the road to decision.

We do all of our travelling following the light of Jesus Christ.

The candle on the table is lit.

ROCKS ON THE PATH

O God, who loves us as we try to tread your way,
the failures in our past lie like rocks on our path,
sometimes stopping us moving as we are filled with guilt and remorse.

A rock is lifted up and placed on the cloth where it touches the ground at the foot of the table.

We confess that we sometimes wish
that you would make things much clearer for us.
Sometimes we even wish that we did not have so much freedom to choose.

Silent reflection

Whether we are young or older,
we have made mistakes in our choosing –
mistakes about what is right or wrong,
about speaking or remaining silent,
about what we want to value in life
and what we want to lay aside.

Silent reflection

Forgive us, loving God.
**Forgive us, O God,
as we place our failures before your cross.**

Amen.

The rock is placed on the table before the cross.

ASSURANCE OF FORGIVENESS

The cross of Jesus is the sign of the costly love of God for all people.
We are never condemned but are offered healing, forgiveness and grace.
Rise up and walk on in faith!

Thanks be to God!

READINGS

There are many guides for Christians on the way.
The word of God in the Bible is one.
The Bible is lifted up.

First Reading

Psalm 119:33-40, 105
In this is the word of God.
Thanks be to God.

Second Reading

Matthew 4:18-23
This is the gospel of Jesus Christ.
Praise to you, Lord Jesus Christ.

The Bible is placed on the cloth where it comes down the aisle.

REFLECTION

- From the day we are born we make choices but, at least when we are children, there is often some guidance around our choices by people who are older and more experienced and who assume some responsibility for what we do and what happens to us.

- However, even as young people we are now seeing many issues before us which involve choices, some harder than others. There are choices about

  lifestyle
  what is right and what is wrong
  career
  relationships
  politics
  and how we view the world
  and what we believe.

- Probably the disciples then had little understanding of what it would mean to follow Jesus, when they answered his call and left their nets.

So, how do Christians make decisions?

- We look into the Bible.

  Our search most of all is to see who God is and to measure that God alongside our hopes for the way we live as people.

  We learn from the insights of our scholars down the ages who tell us more about the times when the Bible was written and the ancient languages and writers.

  None of this takes way from the exciting and inspiring nature of the Holy Bible.

  Because we know that we are to worship God with our whole mind as well as heart and souls and strength, we know that God wants us to address the Bible with our minds.

- We look at the traditions of the church
  as it tries to respond to the living God over the centuries in following its Christ.

- Then because the present church is the body of Christ, we are encouraged to test our ideas with other people.

- We listen to what sound like the prophetic voices of our day – those who challenge what is happening and, usually at some cost to themselves, take their stand.

  We can always look back and see which are the true prophets; it is much harder to see them in the present.

  One of the clues about this was given by Jesus who said, 'By their fruits you will know them'.

- All through this process, we pray to God for wisdom and truth.

- Then we act in faith, and the miracle of grace is that God deeply understands this tough journey and forgives us when we make the wrong choice, holds us close when we fall down in life, gives us a new start every day of our lives and every moment.

- And the wonder is that as we live passionately and joyfully and authentically along this path, sometimes others will be attracted to our fullness of life and join us on the journey with Jesus Christ.

We will become fishers of people, as the disciples did.

FOLLOWING JESUS

The footprints of Jesus do not stay in the sanctuary
but down the mountains into the centre of life,
ready to travel with us through everything we face.

Footprints are placed leading down from the table onto the floor.

As we walk, we gather around us the past tradition of the churches,
and our present companions in the faith.
We listen to the voices of the poor and oppressed,
because Jesus says that our pathway to the truth always includes them.

Silent reflection

THE OFFERING

We share with those crying out on our pathway through life
in working for justice and with our offering.

OFFERING PRAYER

Receive our offerings, loving God,
and carry them into the world which you so love
as a sign that new choices of compassion and justice
are possible for us all.

Amen.

PRAYERS FOR OTHERS AND OURSELVES

God, who stands at the crossroads of life as we make our choices,
we pray for your guidance in all that we do.
Give to us the courage and wisdom to choose your way for us,
that we may more truly be your people.
We pray for those young people among us
who are making critical decisions for the direction of their lives.
Be beside them as they do this, loving Jesus.

Silent prayer

We also remember others today,
especially those who hold great responsibility

for the peoples of the world.
We pray for our own political leaders
as they make choices on our behalf.
May they be just and true, merciful and ethical,
so that we create here a place of kindness
and community for all people.

Silent prayer

Bless all of us here,
that we may grow and learn together
in ways which make our choices easier.
We ask this in the name of Jesus Christ.

Amen.

THE SENDING OUT OF THE PEOPLE OF GOD

The good news for us is that, in walking the pathway of life,
making our difficult choices,
we are always surrounded by the grace of God
and the light of Christ shines ahead of us.

The candle is carried along the cloth down the aisle to the doorway.

BLESSING

Go in faith. Go in peace.
And may the Holy God surprise you on the way,
Christ Jesus take you by the hand,
and the Spirit surround you with a cloud of grace.

Amen.

WALKING AND TALKING TOGETHER

For this service, you will need:
A candle
Flower stickers (from stationers or craft shops)
which are stapled to each order of service

GREETING
Christ be with you.
And also with you.

CALL TO WORSHIP
Jesus Christ, God who walks with us in family and friends,

you are our God.

Great Creator, who speaks to us in unexpected places,

you are our God.

Holy Spirit, who calls us on in truth,

you are our God.
We worship you this day.

A candle is lit.

CONFESSION
Dear God, we are sorry
when we are not the people you would like us to be.
We are sorry when we try to live all by ourselves
instead of talking with you
and with other people who love us.
We are also sorry when we push away other people
who need us to listen to their worries
and to support them in their lives.

Forgive us, loving God,
and help us to love others as you love us.

Amen.

ASSURANCE OF FORGIVENESS

Christ Jesus came into the world to forgive people just like us.
Nothing can separate us from the love of God.
We are forgiven!
Thanks be to God.

READINGS

First Reading
Psalm 117
In this is the word of God.
Thanks be to God.

Second Reading
Luke 24:13-35
This is the gospel of Jesus Christ.
Praise to you, Lord Jesus Christ.

REFLECTION

This time, when I read the story of the people on the road to Emmaus, it
struck me that most of our real questioning happens when we are on the
road – when we are moving from one place to another in our lives or when
we are out and about trying to live from the gospel and finding that not easy.

If the church is really grappling with living out the gospel in the world, the
questions come thick and fast. If it gathers people to it who are varied, with
different histories, who are in some struggle to survive, then the questions
never stop and it is hard to hold it all together. Often children and young
people will ask the real questions and, if we will listen, we will all grow in faith
and understanding as we work things out together.

As people talk anxiously with each other, there are almost always those
who say they have already seen Jesus and others who seem to go to the
same place or live the same sort of life and can't see Jesus present and risen.

Jesus meets us at different places on the road – sometimes by the tomb, sometimes as we walk.

The world outside the church is often very much on the road. The community around us often senses that it would be good to go home, to take the One who seems to be accompanying the journey home to stay towards the night when the questions sometimes become even sharper. Can you imagine taking Jesus home for a good talk? I would love to do that. I wonder what we would each ask? It is good to think about that.

I wonder when we have had moments like this on the road and as the bread is broken – those surprising gifts of understanding, of insight, of restoration of faith. The gospel for us today is that they may be given at any time, in the centre of our anxious questions.

Always those moments are there for us somewhere – possibly as we journey along and sometimes right beside us at the table. Sometimes it is our closest friends and family who talk with us in special ways and sometimes it is a stranger.

CELEBRATING FRIENDS

Attached to your order of service, you were given a flower sticker.
Take that sticker now and put it on the back of your hand.
Hold that hand in your other hand
as though you are holding something very valuable.
In the silence, look at the flower and think of your dearest friend
and all that friend offers to you in love and wisdom and kindness.

A silence is kept.

Let us give thanks to God.
Thank you for all our friends and members of our families
who share our lives and help us to grow in many ways.
We thank you for your friendship too, O God.

Amen.

OFFERING

OFFERING PRAYER

Dear God, as your early friends offered you a meal,
we bring these gifts for people, for families and children
who may need care from us.

Amen.

PRAYERS FOR OTHERS

Dear God, we know that prayer is our way of talking with you.
Sometimes we wish that we could see your face as we speak,
but we believe that you are there listening to us.
We share with you today
that there are many people around the world who need your love.

**Be close to them, O God,
and show us how we can be their friends too.**

Today we remember children who do not have enough to eat,
and children who are afraid or alone
because there is war around them.
We remember families who are trying to find a home,
who may feel that no-one wants to be their friends.

**Be close to them, O God,
and show us how we can be their friends too.**

Then we pray for ourselves,
for all the children here
and for their parents and teachers.

**Keep us safe in your love, O God.
We pray this in your name.**

Amen.

LORD'S PRAYER

**Our Father in heaven,
hallowed be your name,
your kingdom come,
your will be done,**

on earth as in heaven.
Give us today our daily bread.
Forgive us our sins
as we forgive those who sin against us.
Save us from the time of trial
and deliver us from evil.
For the kingdom, the power and the glory are yours
now and for ever. Amen.

DISMISSAL AND BLESSING

Go in peace to find the love of Jesus Christ
among family and friends at every turn in the road.
And may the love of God be our guide,
the courage of Jesus Christ lead us on,
and the Holy Spirit dance ahead of us on the way.

Amen.

FOR PARENTS AND TEACHERS

IN THE BEGINNING

This is a service for staff at the beginning of the school year. It includes a way of welcoming new staff. It could be used as the beginning of the work of any group of people.

For this service, you will need:
A candle and the means of lighting it
A frame with open webbing or netting through which strands of colour can be woven
A basket holding a variety of threads, ribbons, or pieces of fabric

GREETING
Christ be with you.
And also with you.

OPENING SENTENCES
In the beginning,
there was nothing but God
and from that nothingness
arose the miracle of universal life.
In our beginnings,
as we enter a new year,
God lies in the empty spaces,
bringing light to the things that have gone before.

The candle is lit.

Then God goes on,
spreading life beyond where we have been,
shining light into the unknown,
and always creating the wonder of newness for us.
Let us worship God.

LAYING DOWN THE PAST

All of us carry with us past experiences,
past failures or mistakes,
which sometimes lie like burdens in our lives.
All of us have histories in relationships,
things which we wish we had not done or said,
or which should have happened, but never did,
and which we often believe will diminish our future together.
In the silence, let us reflect
on things we would rather not carry into this year.

A silence is kept.

Take all these our burdens into your life, O God.

**We lay them down in faith
for healing, forgiveness, recreation and release.**

Amen.

ASSURANCE

Hear the word of God for us:
'See, the former things have come to pass
and new things I now declare;
before they break from the bud, I announce them to you'.
Rise up and live in hope. Grace is ours this day.

Amen.

READINGS

Isaiah 42:5-9
John 1:1-5

REFLECTION

- There are two central beliefs to the Christian faith and they are intrinsic to new beginnings.
- We believe in a God who lived within our life, within our very body and trod the path of life of humankind.

Therefore this God deeply understands all that we face and every failure and grief is covered with absolute grace and kindness.

- The belief that Jesus 'saves us from our sins' is not necessary about a God who demands a sacrifice of death before forgiveness is offered – that is a primitive spin-off from ancient practices and always sustains an underlying harsh God who demands that sacrifice.

- Could it rather be about a God who so loves us that this God, in a very costly way, absorbs all our pain and grief and guilt into God's own life – into God's own body for healing, grace, comfort and renewal so that we do not need to carry loads from the past on with us as paralysing and disabling burdens? The church, as the body of Christ, at its best, joins with God in that gracious act.

- The second is that this God calls us to tread into an unknown future in faith and, before our eyes, lives out the paradox that lies at the centre of all existence. This is that, as we walk firmly towards things that we fear, things that challenge us, even though that feels like death, in fact the mystery of stronger life lies at the other side.

- We are invited to hear the gospel of Jesus Christ and to lay down any burdens from the past we may be carrying and to so live that we engage with a God who invites us all into a rich and passionate adventure, a life that is full of colour and courage – like a weaving.

WEAVING THE FUTURE TOGETHER

It has become a tradition in this service
to add to the weaving of life and gifts from the past
in the welcoming of new people into our midst.
Our life together in the past has been woven in colour and texture
by all who participate.

Each person adds to the weaving with the colour of their own gifts and skills and their own unique life.

These people are new among us and I now invite them to come forward as I name them and to add their colour to the weaving which we have been creating over the years.

Those named come forward, select a fabric or thread and add it to the weaving.

NEW THREADS IN A WEAVING

(A commitment by new staff or group members)

We dedicate our work to God,
like new threads in a weaving of life.

Go with us into our new year, O God.
Take all that we offer and add to that your gifts.
Breathe into our work your energy, truth and courage,
that we may be faithful, humble people
who are truly gracious to all with whom we work
and committed to the vision of life
with which you call us forward.

WEAVING THE FUTURE

(said by all)

In this new beginning,
in faith we claim our life together,
full with the gifts of God
and the sharing of our gifts,
empty of pride because we stand before God's holiness,
searching in our journey towards deeper truth,
empowered by the life of the Spirit among us
and the friendship of Jesus Christ.
In faith we commit ourselves
to the care for each person who is here,
to the well-being of the whole,
to a greater dream for the new year,
woven in many colours and drawn in creative beauty
through the community we share
in the grand adventure of being your people.

SENDING OUT AND BLESSING

Go in peace into the tasks and relationships that lie ahead.
Go in faith because we never travel alone.
God is with us and we are with each other.

And may you tread in the footsteps of the Christ,
safely walking on the rock which is our God,
and be covered by the warm bright wings of the Holy Spirit.

Amen.

PASSING ON THE MANTLE OF CARE

A Service for parents of Children who are beginning life at a new school or Sunday school.

For this service, you will need:
A beautiful scarf or shawl

CALL TO WORSHIP

God, who is the loving parent of all humankind,
God, who sent the Son Jesus to save us,
God who gives birth to new possibilities
through the Holy Spirit who never leaves us,

we worship you, in Spirit and in truth.

PRAYER OF CONFESSION

Loving God,
you know it is not always easy to be a parent.
Sometimes we find it hard to hold the balance
between giving our children freedom
and the exercising of our own responsibilities.
Sometimes we are tempted
to hold our children too tightly to us
as we try to save them from the pain and risks of life.

Silent reflection

Then, dear God, most of us have times
when our patience is stretched thin,
or when we would simply like a rest from being parents.
All of us do things we regret or fail to do things we should do.

Silent reflection

We ask your forgiveness, O God,
for we are always dependent on your grace.

Amen.

ASSURANCE OF PARDON

Hear the good news for us in Jesus Christ:
nothing can separate us from the love of God.
We are forgiven!

Thanks be to God.

READINGS

First Reading
Psalm 121
In this is the word of God.
Thanks be to God.

Second Reading
Luke 2:41-47
This is the gospel of the Lord.
Praise be to you, Lord Jesus Christ.

REFLECTION

- We know very little about the childhood of Jesus, other than this account of when he stayed behind with the teachers in the synagogue and his parents lost him for a while.

- He was obviously an exceptional child and grew in grace and learning.

- We all hope that for our children and often find that we must entrust them to the care of others at regular stages of their growing.

- Entrusting others with the development of the very heart and soul of our children as we teach them the faith is a major thing to do – an act of trust and faith in itself.

- Jesus obviously loved little children and warned those who would harm or deprive them.

- As you make your own commitment to enhance the growing of your children in life and faith here today, I know that those who receive your trust will take their task with grave responsibility.

· We all need each others' prayers as parents and as teachers. None of us underestimates the sacred task we have been given.

THE MANTLE OF RESPONSIBILITY AND CARE

I now invite you as parents to ask the principal of the school
(or representative Sunday school teacher)
to assume the mantle of care and responsibility for your children.

The parents say:

In faith and hope,
we invite you to assume a mantle of responsibility
for the education of these, our loved children.
We place it upon your shoulders as a sacred trust,
the sacred trust of sharing with us
in the guiding of each unique child
towards wisdom and learning,
maturity and wholeness
in an environment of care.

The principal or teacher comes forward and the mantle is placed on her/his shoulders.
The principal or teacher says:

I receive this mantle with a sense of grave responsibility.
I commit myself and this school (Sunday school)
to the care of your children.
By the grace of God,
we will cherish them each day.
We will work to create for them
a safe, compassionate and respectful place
for their growing and learning
in a spirit of true community
with each other and the world.

PRAYERS OF INTERCESSION

God of grace, take all that we offer
and add to it the gifts of your holy life.
Be with the staff of this school and all its students,
and with those of us who are parents.
Carry us into a year of true creativity in all that is good.
Walk with us in wonder as we watch
the unfolding life of our children
and give to us all that we need in faith and hope as we go.
Be with all children, especially those whose needs are great
and resources small.

Amen.

HYMN

SENDING OUT AND BLESSING

Go in peace into the adventure of life.
And may the holy God hold you firm,
Christ Jesus take you by the hand,
and the Holy Spirit be a cloud of grace around you.

Amen.

The Society for Promoting Christian Knowledge (SPCK) was
founded in 1698. Its mission statement is:

To promote Christian knowledge by

- **Communicating the Christian faith in its
  rich diversity;**
- **Helping people to understand the Christian faith
  and to develop their personal faith; and**
- **Equipping Christians for mission and ministry.**

SPCK Worldwide serves the Church through Christian
literature and communication projects in over 100 countries, and
provides books for those training for ministry in many parts of
the developing world. This worldwide service depends upon the
generosity of others and all gifts are spent wholly on ministry
programmes, without deductions.

SPCK Bookshops support the life of the Christian community
by making available a full range of Christian literature and other
resources, providing support for those training for ministry, and
assisting bookstalls and book agents throughout the UK.

SPCK Publishing produces Christian books and resources,
covering a wide range of inspirational, pastoral, practical and
academic subjects. Authors are drawn from many different
Christian traditions, and publications aim to meet the needs of a
wide variety of readers in the UK and throughout the world.

The Society does not necessarily endorse the individual views
contained in its publications, but hopes they stimulate readers to
think about and further develop their Christian faith.

For further information about the Society, visit our website at
www.spck.org.uk or write to:
SPCK, 36 Causton Street,
London SW1P 4ST, United Kingdom.